D0801609

TRUE CRIME :
NEW JERSEY

TRUE CRIME : NEW JERSEY

The State's Most Notorious Criminal Cases

Patricia A. Martinelli

STACKPOLE
BOOKS

Published by
STACKPOLE BOOKS
5067 Ritter Road
Mechanicsburg, PA 17055
www.stackpolebooks.com

Printed in the United States of America

10 9 8 7 6 5 4 3 2

FIRST EDITION

Cover design by Caroline Stover
Photo of handgun on cover ©Lew Robertson/Corbis

Library of Congress Cataloging-in-Publication Data

Martinelli, Patricia A.
    True crime : New Jersey: the state's most notorious criminal cases / Patricia A. Martinelli. — 1st ed.
        p. cm.
    Includes bibliographical references.
    ISBN-13: 978-0-8117-3428-8 (pbk.)
    ISBN-10: 0-8117-3428-5 (pbk.)
    1. Crime—New Jersey—Case studies. 2. Criminals—New Jersey—Case studies. I. Title.
HV6793.N4M37   2007
364.109749—dc22

2007001677

To the memory of my cousin, Jeff Downey,
who loved his family, his friends,
good times, and good stories.
He will live forever in our hearts.

Contents

Introduction

Sex. Violence.

Ask filmmakers about these subjects and they'll likely say that they are two basic ingredients of good movies. But ask victims of serious crimes such as rape or aggravated assault, and chances are good that the only response you'll get will be unprintable. When we watch terrifying films or read scary books, we have a sense of control, as we can stop a movie or set a novel aside if the action starts to get too intense. But in real life, the victims of violent crimes don't have easy access to a reverse or pause button.

Modern society seems filled with graphic, sometimes disturbing images that would not have been allowed in public a generation ago. Are gory movies and violent music lyrics at least partially responsible for why there seem to be so many random acts of violence nowadays? Although the media often trumpets such incidents as signaling the end of civilization, social commentators and trained psychologists have yet to fully determine the answers to these difficult questions. History has shown that violent, predatory behavior has occurred repeatedly over the centuries throughout human civilization, in different cultures around the world. As a result, it is not always easy to tell if modern life is, as Charles Dickens once stated, the best of times or the worst of times.

As in the rest of America, New Jersey residents are plagued by everything from destructive pranks to brutal assaults and murders. In some instances, rejected spouses or ex-lovers prefer to kill the object of their affection rather than allow that person to love someone else. Sometimes a person just has the misfortune of being in the wrong place at the wrong time. Children disappear from the security of their

CRIME BY THE NUMBERS

For the past four decades, the New Jersey State Police Department has compiled facts and figures about crime in the Garden State. The most frightening statistic appears to be the fact that though the population hasn't increased all that much since 1960, rising from a little over 6 million to more than 8 million residents, incidents of almost all types of crime have risen dramatically.

For example, in 1960, the state police documented 164 murders, 442 incidents of rape, 2,591 robberies, and 3,735 assaults. Ten years later, although the state's population had increased by only about 1 million people, the number of murders had almost quadrupled, to 412. Other crimes also increased, with 927 reported rapes, 12,145 robberies, and 7,099 assaults.

For the most part, the figures continued to climb over the years. By 2000, with the state's population hovering at more than 8 million, the state police files included 1,357 rapes, 13,553 robberies, and 17,099 assaults. The only statistic to show any significant decrease was that for murder, which dropped to 289.

One factor that may have played a major role in the increase in robberies is drug use, since addicts will steal almost anything in order to raise money to buy what they need to stay high. Another may simply be the proximity of too many people, which creates additional stress in an already fast-paced world. Although it ranks ninth in population for the United States, New Jersey is the most densely populated state in the entire country.

homes, never to be seen alive again. Family members and friends of victims find their lives irreparably damaged as they wrestle to understand the tragedies, often wondering whether they would have been able to avert the outcome if they had only done or said something a little sooner. Homeowners install alarm systems, security cameras, and other devices in hopes of making life safer. But when they turn on the evening news and witness some of the violent incidents that have occurred for no apparent reason, these precautions just don't seem like enough.

New Jersey residents may have good reason to worry. Crime statistics kept by the New Jersey State Police indicate that while the number of reported murders has dropped, violence in the Garden State has increased dramatically in recent years. In 2005, Camden claimed the top spot as America's most dangerous city for the second year in a row, beating Detroit and other serious contenders for that dubious honor. It had the highest violent crime, murder, and robbery rates among all American cities with a population of at least 75,000 people. Though municipal officials claim that the statistics cited in the annual *City Crime Rankings* are out-of-date and misleading, Morgan Quitno Press, the publishers of the book, state that their research accurately reflects life in Camden today.

Crime is not limited to New Jersey's cities, however. Police officers throughout the state never know what awaits them when they clock in to begin their shift, even in the smallest towns. Both state and local police officers all too often find themselves confronted by suspects who have little or no apparent fear of authority. Limited staffing and shrinking equipment budgets sometimes make it difficult for the police to be as effective as they'd like to be in the performance of their duties.

Research for this book led me back through state history into the lives of various villains, with an assortment of heinous acts that will probably continue to cause me many sleepless nights in the future. But it was necessary to look at the overall picture of crime past and present in New Jersey in order to select the most relevant examples for discussion. The purpose of this book is not to examine minor offenses or moral dilemmas. Rather, it gives a sample of some of New Jersey's most famous criminal cases and examines such topics as kidnapping, organized crime, and murder. The more detailed accounts are interspersed with brief outlines of other, less familiar cases that occurred in the Garden State. Although many cases were readily solved, some remain a mystery more than a century later.

The crimes are presented in chronological order, beginning with the Lindbergh kidnapping, a story that became national news long before cable television networks were around to provide round-the-clock coverage of such events. The stories continue from the early twentieth century to the present day. Though each case is unique, they all seem disturbingly familiar. Anyone who reads a newspaper or listens to the nightly news will soon realize that we've been down most of these dark and lonely roads before.

The legal definitions of certain crimes have changed somewhat over the generations. Once, not so long ago, a man could be hanged if he were convicted of stealing another man's horse. Women who dared to protest their lack of rights to own property and to vote could be jailed for creating a public disturbance. The charge of witchcraft could be leveled at just about anyone, and the accused were often brutally tested before judgment was passed. In some towns, it was a violation to sell liquor or conduct business on a Sunday, and in some cases it still is. As a result, to better understand the crimes that are recounted in this book, it is necessary to look back through the centuries for a quick overview of the darker side of life in the Garden State.

CHAPTER 1

A Brief History of Crime in New Jersey

✳ ✳ ✳

It would be impossible to provide an in-depth look at all of the crimes that have occurred in New Jersey since its earliest days of known settlement by the Lenni-Lenape, who resided in the region before the arrival of European immigrants. Respected as a peaceful people, these Native Americans sometimes found it necessary to protect themselves from other, more warlike tribes who wanted access to the state's vast forests and pristine waterways. Though disputes over the region's rich resources were sometimes settled in battle, it was not until the arrival of the wooden sailing ships from various European ports that the tribes found themselves increasingly at risk in the territory that had long been their home.

It is believed that two Indians were responsible for the first recorded murders in New Jersey, at a time when the territory was still a colony. In the 1670s, two braves named Tashiowycan and Wyannattamo, from the central portion of the territory, reportedly killed two Dutchmen who worked at the trading post on Burlington Island, a 300-acre patch of land that sits in the Delaware River. One account stated that the Indians allegedly were determined to avenge the death of Tashiowycan's sister, but it gives no further details on why they decided that these two particular settlers were involved in the young woman's demise. According to another report, the two tribesmen were drunk when they killed the settlers. Whatever the reason, when the murders of the Dutchmen were discovered, tensions grew strained between the Native Americans and the colonists. To restore peace, tribal leaders were believed to have ordered the death of the two Indians responsible for the crime.

About ten years later, the arrival of William Penn and his company of Quakers stabilized the relationship between the newcomers and the natives, but even Penn's treaties were not always a guarantee against violence by one side against the other. Tensions continued to grow as more and more colonists flocked to the New World. By the middle of the eighteenth century, when the French and Indian Wars erupted, some Native Americans were only too ready to help the French kill English settlers in an effort to stop Britain's expansion throughout the colonies. Their actions sometimes provoked a deadly response.

After Indians murdered his family during the wars, a formerly peace-loving immigrant named Tom Quick went on a rampage in what is now northwestern New Jersey, killing as many natives as he could find. Although taking the law into your own hands was common in those days, state officials soon branded him a criminal. They were concerned that Quick's actions would cause the tenuous relations between the Native Americans and the colonists, which had calmed after the wars, to completely disintegrate. But when they attempted to arrest him on murder charges, Quick escaped and went into hiding. He reportedly died in bed of small-pox years later, but he was not destined to rest peacefully. After he was buried, the local tribes dug up his body and ceremoniously burned it to make sure he was really dead. As a result, they only managed to complete Quick's vendetta for him, as the smoke spread the pox quickly among the Native Americans, almost wiping out the region's remaining population.

As new arrivals from Europe continued to flood the American colonies, most of the surviving Lenni-Lenape moved westward. But their departure simply meant that the settlers preyed on each other instead of the Native Americans. During the seventeenth and eighteenth centuries, the justice system in the regions that came to be known as East Jersey and West Jersey was strongly influenced by England, whose wealthy aristocrats owned much of the land. The British legal system at that time decreed swift and merciless punishment for most offenders, no matter how small the crime. Theft, whether of a loaf of bread or money, was considered a capital crime that often resulted in hanging. Credit for large and small purchases was easily obtainable, but woe to those who failed to pay when their notes came due. Debtors often found themselves in prison, where, ironically enough, they were supposed to pay for their food and shelter. Occasionally, if no other alternative was available, some chose to become indentured servants to their creditors to work off the debt. But many people found themselves incarcerated for years before the money was raised to purchase their freedom. It wasn't until the nineteenth century that authorities realized the system of mass imprisonment was reducing a valuable labor force, and the laws concerning debt began to change.

By the late 1700s, however, many American colonists began to notice that a number of existing laws no longer seemed suitable for their fledgling country. When their request for adequate representation was ignored by the British crown, the settlers not only broke the laws, they broke away from foreign rule. Unfortunately, the fight for freedom against England occasionally brought out the worst in the settlers. The advent of the Revolutionary War saw greedy politicians and merchants inflate the cost of food or stockpile goods needed by local citizens. Theft was rampant, as Americans raided or captured British supply boats and sold their cargo—and sometimes the ships—at auction. When the conflict was over, not everyone was nobly concerned with the welfare of the newly formed United States of America. *New Jersey: A Guide to Its Present and Past,* published in 1946 by the Works Progress Administration, tells of a gang of counterfeiters that occupied a house in Paulsboro shortly after the Revolutionary War ended. There they produced fake bonds and money that were successfully circulated throughout the state before they were captured by the authorities.

Counterfeiters were not the only criminals roaming the state in those early days. In the tiny hamlet of Shacks Corner, west of Hamilton, an old tavern served as the headquarters of a man named Fenton, an outlaw who haunted the Pine Barrens. One of many such highwaymen who hid from the law in the vast, unsettled region, Fenton was eventually arrested by the Monmouth County militia, who shot him, then hung his body from a tree outside the courthouse in Freehold as a warning to other outlaws. Another well-known highwayman was Joe Mulliner, who terrorized both American patriots and British Loyalists in the forests around the rural ironmaking community of Batsto. Captured in 1781, he was believed to have been hanged outside the courthouse in Burlington City, which was the region's capital at that time. Although such speedy punishment might seem harsh by modern standards, for many outlaws it may have been preferable to the alternative.

Prisons were frightening places in those early days. Dank, dark, and disease-ridden, they physically reflected society's attitude toward lawbreakers. No one cared whether inmates were rehabilitated. The only concern was that they be imprisoned and punished for what they had done wrong. While fortresslike, intimidating structures were usually located in major cities, rural communities often used small jails designed to hold just three or four offenders.

When Cumberland officially became a county in January 1748, one of the first decisions of the newly elected Board of Chosen Freeholders was to build a stronger jail than the old wooden one, from which prisoners repeatedly escaped. According to the Freeholders' meeting minutes dated March 24 of that year, "At a special meeting of the Justices and Freeholders they unanimously agreed that the said county do build a gaol at the most convenient place do shall think proper for the benefit of said county the dimension of which to be about twelve feet square the above said gaol." Like those in just about every New Jersey county, Cumberland's jail continued to grow larger as the years passed and the population increased. Less than fifty years later, an expansion was proposed that included cells for debtors and criminals, as well as a dungeon that measured twelve feet square.

On February 15, 1798, the state of New Jersey passed a supplement to "an act making provisions for carrying into effect the act for the punishment of crimes." Included in the guidelines for managing prisoners was a section stating that "the greatest offenders be confined at night in the solitary cells, separately, so far as the vacant cells will permit, and that the daily allowance of each prisoner confined in the yard, shall be one pound of coarse bread, half a pound of animal flesh made into soup, with plenty of vegetables, and one gill of molasses." Although this diet might seem insufficient now, it was in fact not much different—and sometimes more substantial—than that of most of the working class and the poor.

It will probably come as no surprise that prominent figures, then as now, were not always sent to prison or subjected to the same punishment as the average person. One such person was Aaron Burr, vice president to Thomas Jefferson, whose political ambitions ultimately drove a wedge between him and other significant figures of the day. Tension between Burr and his longtime nemesis, Secretary of the Treasury Alexander Hamilton, finally exploded on July 11, 1804, when the two men fought a duel in Weehawken. Burr fatally wounded Hamilton, who died the following day, but authorities in both New Jersey and New York were never able to apprehend the vice president on a charge of murder. After disappearing for a time from political circles, Burr eventually returned to Washington, D.C., to finish his term of office. Like many criminals, however, he apparently had not learned from his narrow escape and eventually was brought to trial for a variety of other serious charges, including treason and corruption. It seems that the former vice president of the United States had conspired with others to overthrow American interests in the western territories and create an empire that he planned to rule. Burr escaped conviction once again by voluntarily exiling himself to Europe for a while, and after returning to America, finished his days as a lawyer in New York. The man who once aspired to lead a nation died in 1836 at age eighty and was buried in Princeton Cemetery.

On March 19, 1875, New Jersey entrepreneur Charles K. Landis, who had amassed a fortune through his real estate and railroad ventures, strolled into the downtown office of the *Vineland Independent* and shot editor Uri Carruth in the back of the head. Landis was outraged because Carruth apparently had printed an article that portrayed him as a coldhearted villain who was planning to have his wife committed to an insane asylum. When Landis, the founder of Hammonton and Vineland, was brought to trial the following January, the case was extensively covered by newspapers all along the East Coast. But Landis's attorney mounted a successful defense against the charge. His client was found not guilty by reason of temporary insanity and was never sent to prison.

Other criminals, successfully tried and convicted of their crimes at different times, were not as fortunate as Burr and Landis. In the early days, those who were not hanged endured imprisonment, hard labor, public whippings, and other forms of torture that were considered appropriate punishment by the legal system at that time. By the nineteenth century, however, New Jersey authorities began to seriously reconsider how prisoners were treated and examine methods of incarceration that had been, up until that time, commonly accepted in both the New World and the Old. One example of changing attitudes can be seen at the Mount Holly Jail, also known as Burlington County Prison, which opened its doors in 1808 and continued to house prisoners for more than 150 years. Designed by architect Robert Mills, who was a friend of Thomas Jefferson, the three-story, gray stone building was supposed to offer inmates less physically intimidating surroundings and some creature comforts not always found at other prisons. Regulations required that each inmate be bathed and deloused upon arrival, and their clothes were fumigated to reduce the spread of disease. Every man had his own cell, complete with a window at eye level and a fireplace, as well as a prayer book or Bible for spiritual instruction. The solitude was supposed to keep the prisoners from the corrupting influences of others and give them time to repent of their crimes.

Although these things were considered social improvements, some inmates still preferred to take their chances in the outside world. According to the informational brochure offered to visitors who tour the facility today: "One notable escape occurred in 1875. A hole was punched through the ceiling of an upper corridor cell to gain access to the roof and the escape of four men was made good by climbing down a woodpile next to the prison yard wall. A fifth accomplice, too large to fit through the hole and incensed at being left behind, reportedly sounded the alarm. Despite a quick response by the warden, it seems that at least some of these escapees were never caught." Mills, who later designed part of Independence Hall, the Washington Monument, and other structures, was considered a radical for creating such an unusual prison. But in the years that followed, his ideas and those of other reformers were slowly adopted by a society that began to believe even hardened offenders could be rehabilitated.

Did such farsighted changes reduce the amount of violence in New Jersey? Hardly. During the nineteenth century, the crimes were as diverse as the population that continued to expand throughout the state. In 1833, a French immigrant named Antoine LeBlanc was charged with murdering Samuel Sayre, a wealthy Morristown resident who had hired LeBlanc to work as a gardener. After a week of trimming and planting, the Frenchman, apparently jealous of their wealth, murdered Sayre, his wife Sarah, and their servant Phoebe, and hid their bodies in the barn. LeBlanc then robbed the house, but he was captured shortly after committing the heinous crime. The entire nation, shocked by his deeds, read every lurid detail in the "penny press," as cheap, sensationalistic brochures—the predecessors of today's tabloids—were then known. One titled *Murder of the Sayre Family at Morristown, New Jersey, by Antoine LeBlanc, May 11, 1833* was published less than a month after the crime. Although he swore that he was innocent, LeBlanc was ultimately tried and hanged for his crimes. His body was later turned over to Dr. Isaac Canfield, a local surgeon, for dissection. Some of his skin was used to make everyday items like a purse that is part of the collections currently owned by the New Jersey Historical Society in Newark.

Women during that period, considered the more delicate sex, were sometimes treated less harshly than men when they committed similar offenses. At the same time, they still received their share of notoriety. In June 1837, the *Philadelphia Inquirer* reported that Mrs. Anne Bowers had died in the lunatic asylum where she had been remanded about six months earlier after she "blew off the top" of her husband's head with a shotgun. According to the brief newspaper account, the couple had been visiting friends in Bridgeton when the incident occurred. Bowers apparently shot her husband, an engineer with the Central Railroad, while he lay sleeping.

Sometimes the criminal was not always captured so easily—or, for that matter, captured at all. One such case was that of Mary Rogers, a "beautiful cigar girl" who lived and worked in New York City. On July 28, 1841, her body was discovered floating in the Hudson River off the shores of Hoboken near a popular recreational spot called Sybil's Cave. As a sales clerk in John Anderson's tobacco store, Rogers was well known to local authors and newspaper reporters who frequented the shop. Speculation about her death remained rife for years: Was she murdered by a street gang? Was it her fiancé? Although a variety of suspects were named during the investigation, no conclusive evidence was ever found to link any of them to the crime. Like the case of Antoine LeBlanc, the mystery of Mary Rogers's death was considered ideal fodder for the penny press, which churned out a new issue every time another lead in the case was disclosed. Edgar Allan Poe, who knew Rogers, memorialized her death in his famous tale titled *The Mystery of Marie Roget.* Like others, he speculated that the young woman had come to New Jersey because she was pregnant and had actually died as the result of a botched abortion at a Hoboken seaside hotel. But to this day, no one has ever satisfactorily resolved the question of who killed the beautiful cigar girl.

During the late nineteenth century, theft was another problem that became commonplace in New Jersey, especially in overcrowded cities. On June 23, 1893, the *Philadelphia Inquirer* reported:

> A bold burglar made a haul of $400 worth of watches from T. L. Bear's jewelry store, 207 Market [S]treet, Camden, early yesterday morning. About 3 o'clock the thief threw a cobblestone through the show window and grabbed twenty watches. The electric light at the street corner and a gas lamp in the store were burning brightly, and a pedestrian saw the thief at work. No policeman could be found and before an officer was secured the burglar escaped. Mr. Bear has offered a reward of $100 for the conviction of the thief, and notified the Philadelphia pawn shops.

As years passed, crime in the Garden State continued to flourish. By the twentieth century, murder, rape, robbery, and assault occurred with increasing regularity in cities and towns throughout the state. Some lawbreakers were jailed, but the death penalty was still commonly used on those convicted of more serious crimes. Public opinion was turning against the use of hanging as the punishment for capital offenses, however. It was not that most people felt criminals shouldn't suffer the ultimate penalty for serious

DEATH TO THE DEATH PENALTY?

Frivolous statutes have long been a part of the history of most states, and New Jersey is no exception. According to www.dumb.com: In Caldwell, you are not allowed to dance or wear shorts in the center of town. And it is illegal in Manville to offer zoo animals whiskey or cigarettes. Other odd laws that are on the books prohibit the slurping of soup, forbid boiling bones on your own property, require cats to wear three bells to warn birds that they are nearby, and bar horse racing from the New Jersey Turnpike.

Of course, Garden State legislators also address more serious issues. In 1982, government officials decided to revive the death penalty to punish criminals convicted of capital crimes such as murder. The death sentence has come under recent attack, however, because it has not been used in more than twenty-five years. Some supporters have dubbed it a "paper lion," as the appeals process allows criminals to sit for years on death row at the New Jersey State Prison in Trenton. Better, some say, to not have it as an option at all than to have it and not use it. Opponents to the death penalty include Gov. Jon Corzine, who assumed office in 2006, so it eventually may be abolished once again. Legislators have created a number of bills in recent years that would eliminate the ultimate penalty and replace it with a life sentence without the possibility of parole.

offenses. The practice was considered too cruel and barbaric because it frequently took a while for the hanged man to die. As a result, the invention of the electric chair was hailed as a more benevolent way to execute criminals. The device was introduced into the penal system around 1906; shortly afterward, it became a fixture on the first "death row" built at the New Jersey State Prison in Trenton. As government became more centralized, the counties often sent hardened criminals there for execution, prompting public out-

Even though four of the inmates currently housed on death row have exhausted all their avenues of appeal, it is unlikely that there will be a lethal injection, the current method used for execution, in the future. In February 2004, the courts decreed that the state could not execute anyone until it revised existing procedures on how the penalty would be imposed. Among the court's apparent concerns were a lack of public access to executions and the state's inability to handle last-second stays of execution. Legislators extended the moratorium until two months after Corzine receives input from a special commission formed in 2006 to study executions in New Jersey. The commission's findings included information on whether the death penalty law is fairly applied, its costs, and whether it has actually deterred crime. New Jersey is the third state to impose a moratorium on the death penalty, after Maryland and Illinois.

A number of organizations, including the Innocence Project for Justice at Rutgers University School of Law, have been campaigning in recent years against the death penalty. "Last year, New Jersey Policy Perspective, a liberal think tank, said the state has spent $253 million in the past 23 years on a death penalty that hasn't been used," according to www .wcbs880.com. Currently, twelve men and one woman are prisoners on death row. For the record, no death row prisoners in New Jersey, which includes Jesse Timmendequas, who raped and murdered seven-year-old Hamilton Township resident Megan Kanka in 1994, have been found innocent of their various crimes.

cry from Trenton residents who did not want other inmates housed at the prison. They ultimately lost the argument.

Built by Carl F. Adams, founder of Adams Electric, the electric chair featured heavy leather straps used to secure the prisoner's arms, ankles, and chest and a metal cap that was fitted above the head. Electrodes, attached to the cap and the prisoner's right leg, conducted electricity through the body. According to Mark Falzini, archivist at the New Jersey State Police Museum in Trenton: "There were three switches, each of which was held for thirty seconds. The first was for 2,400 volts, and the second was for 1,200 volts. After those were pulled, the doctors listened for a pulse and breathing. If they heard something, then a third switch of 600 volts was pulled for thirty seconds."

The first person to be executed in New Jersey's electric chair was Saverio DiGiovanni, a thirty-four-year-old Italian immigrant who was convicted of shooting Joseph Sansome during a dispute. After a month on death row, DiGiovanni was executed on December 11, 1907. More than 150 men, including Bruno Richard Hauptmann, who was convicted of kidnapping the Lindbergh baby, died by electrocution before the death penalty was abolished in the state in 1963. Although it was later reinstated in 1982, with modern-day executions performed by lethal injection, a growing tide of dissent against the death penalty has since caused lawmakers to delay carrying out some sentences or overturn existing convictions altogether. Not a single prisoner on death row in New Jersey has been executed in more than twenty-five years.

During the late nineteenth through the early twentieth century, there was a huge surge in migration from the Old World to the New as living conditions there became increasingly intolerable for the working class. To ease the transition, the newcomers frequently stuck closely together in neighborhoods, and they were often unwilling to trust the authorities when they became the victims of crimes. This problem was especially true for the Italians, who formed one of the largest groups of immigrants to settle in New Jersey. Many of them came from southern Italy, and for the most part, they were hardworking, decent people who, like other arrivals, hoped to find a better way of life in their new homeland. Unfortunately, with them came the centuries-old Mafia, a secret society that ultimately developed into a criminal organization that soon spread its tentacles throughout the state and the country. The New Jersey branches of the crime families initially were not as well known as those in New York and Philadelphia, but they still made their presence felt. Some Italian families in the Garden State readily recalled the threat of the Black Hand, a symbol once reportedly used as a threat by the Mafia to force other immigrants to pay protection for their homes and businesses. Although state and federal officials occasionally managed to jail the mob bosses, they never succeeded in exterminating the syndicate itself. Over the years, organized crime expanded into everything from political corruption to drug trafficking. And one sure source of income in those early days was the sale of alcohol.

When federal lawmakers adopted Prohibition in 1920, illegal stills spread faster than a brush fire through the New Jersey Pine Barrens and other remote locations, providing hard liquor to thirsty residents who willingly chose to disobey what they considered an unjust law. Whether part of an organized crime syndicate or operated independently, the stills supplied what the public demanded. But they weren't the only source of alcohol flooding the state at that time. In *Atlantic City Diary: A Century of Memories, 1880–1985,* author Ed Davis noted that federal authorities were so disturbed by the number of rumrunners smuggling alcohol into Atlantic City that they sent in U.S. District Attorney Frederick W. Pearse to combat the growing tide of lawbreakers. Apparently schooners from the West Indies would anchor offshore, and small boats were used to smuggle the liquor to shore. Davis noted that in addition to pursuing the smugglers, federal officials charged many local café owners and their staffs with buying and selling alcohol.

Liquor was just one of many problems confronting law enforcement officers in New Jersey during the Roaring Twenties, when it seemed as if even the most law-abiding citizens were determined to leave behind the conventions of the Victorian era. A famous criminal case during that period was the scandalous Hall-Mills murders, which, like the death of Mary Rogers, dominated the penny press and public attention for years. On September 16, 1922, the body of Rev. Edward Wheeler Hall, age forty-one, the popular pastor of the Protestant Episcopal Church of St. John the Evangelist in New Brunswick, was found under a crab apple tree in De Russey's Lane. Near him lay the body of his lover, thirty-four-year-old choir singer Eleanor Rinehardt Mills. Hall had been shot, but Mills's corpse had been mutilated as well. Letters from Mills to her hapless lover lay scattered at their feet. Mills's husband, James, ultimately became a suspect but proved to have an alibi for the night of the murder. The pastor's widow, Frances Stevens Hall, age forty-eight, and two of her brothers were eventually tried for the murders, but all three were acquitted. Because they were members of the wealthy and respected Stevens family, other local residents simply could not believe they were involved. So as with the Mary Rogers murder, the mystery of who killed the minister and his alleged lover remains unsolved to this day.

Another murderous drama that unfolded in South Jersey a few years later involved forty-two-year-old Margaret Lilliendahl. In 1927, the Vineland homemaker was tried and convicted of murdering her husband, A. William Lilliendahl, a local physician about twenty years her senior. At first Lilliendahl claimed that her husband had been shot to death on a lonely lane near Hammonton by two black men while he was making his rounds. Authorities later proved that the doctor's murder actually had been prearranged by his wife, assisted by her lover, a poultry farmer named Willis Beach. According to Gerald Tomlinson, author of *Murdered in Jersey,* "Three witnesses, it seemed, had observed Beach jump into his car on the lonely side road not fifty feet from the scene of the murder at the very hour of the crime and take off toward Hammonton." The trial lasted less than two weeks. When it was over, the jury convicted the pair of voluntary manslaughter instead of first-degree murder, believing that the prosecution's case had been based primarily on circumstantial evidence. Both Lilliendahl and Beach were sentenced to ten years of hard labor, but neither was destined to serve the full term. Beach suffered a fatal heart attack less than two years after he was incarcerated at a Bordentown prison farm. Lilliendahl served five years in Trenton State Prison and another two at a women's reformatory in Clinton, but then was released because she reportedly was dying of an incurable disease.

During the 1930s, the entire country reeled from devastating financial difficulties after the resounding stock market crash on October 28, 1929. Black Friday, as the day came to be known, had far-reaching economic implications. Like many Americans, New Jersey residents found themselves caught in the grip of the Great Depression, out of work and with food, gasoline, and other everyday necessities not always readily available. Sigmund Freud may have just written his groundbreaking study titled *Civilization and Its Discontents,* Charlie Chaplin may have been entertaining moviegoers in *City Lights,* but the decade on the whole did not look promising. At the same time, crime was on the upswing. Names like John Dillinger, Bonnie and Clyde, and Ma Barker became familiar to the public as they robbed banks and fought blazing gun battles with the law.

In 1932, the election of Franklin Delano Roosevelt to the office of president of the United States was seen as a positive first step toward economic recovery. But in March of that same year, a devastating event captured the attention of the entire nation, and families throughout the country clutched their children a little closer, when the only son of internationally celebrated pilot Charles Lindbergh was kidnapped from his New Jersey home.

CHAPTER 2
Little Boy Lost

* * *

It began with an empty crib and a ransom note discovered on a blustery night in 1932. It should have ended with the death of a convicted criminal. But for many, the tragedy that occurred to the family of noted American aviator Charles Lindbergh still remains far from resolved.

Charles Augustus Lindbergh was christened "Lucky Lindy" by the media after he became the first pilot to successfully cross the Atlantic Ocean all alone on May 20–21, 1927. His journey captured the nation's imagination because the concept of air travel was still so new at that time, and only a few teams of men had been heroic enough to risk the journey prior to his flight. Suddenly everyone wanted to know: Who was this daring young man in the "flying machine"? Could it really have been the shy, studious midwestern youth who early on had showed an aptitude for mechanics?

Lindbergh was born on February 2, 1902, in Detroit to Charles Sr., a successful attorney and U.S. congressman, and Evangeline Lodge Land Lindbergh. Raised on a farm near Little Falls, Minnesota, he was accepted to the University of Wisconsin after graduating from high school. He began to study engineering in college, but Lindbergh soon realized he wasn't destined to make his living in such a traditional way. Beneath his placid exterior, the young man harbored the spirit of an adventurer. Two years after he started, Lindbergh left the quiet of the classroom for life on the road as a barnstormer, a pilot who performed aerial stunts at county fairs. Although he continued to show a flair for engineering throughout his life, Lindbergh's first love would always be flying.

In 1927, he decided to accept the challenge originally issued almost a decade before by New York City hotel owner Raymond Orteig. According to www.charleslindbergh.com, a website dedicated to Lindbergh's memory, the lure was "$25,000 to the first aviator to fly nonstop from New York to Paris. Several pilots were killed or injured while competing for the Orteig prize. By 1927, it had still not been won. Lindbergh believed he could win it if he had the right airplane." With a cartel of St. Louis businessmen as his sponsors, Lindbergh designed a plane that was built by Ryan Aeronautical Company of San Diego. He christened it the *Spirit of St. Louis,* and as a test, he flew from San Diego to New York City, setting a transcontinental record of twenty hours and twenty-one minutes. Encouraged, he decided to accept the gauntlet thrown down by Orteig and made the 3,600-mile journey across the Atlantic Ocean in less than thirty-three and a half hours.

Lindbergh's achievement was applauded throughout the United States and Europe. He was the guest of honor in countless parades and ceremonies and received both the Medal of Honor and the Distinguished Flying Cross from President Calvin Coolidge. Following his momentous solo victory, the young pilot joined the fledgling U.S. Army Air Corps and eventually attained the rank of colonel. As one of the small number of men who had entered the field, Lindbergh found his services in high demand. He traveled extensively as an aviation consultant, and with his support, the fledgling airline industry soon gained new acceptance by the American public. Before long, planes were carrying both air mail and passengers, who marveled at the idea of traveling by means that seemed like something straight out of *Flash Gordon,* the popular sci-fi cliff-hanger that ran each week at the local movie theater. Ironically, Lindbergh's chosen occupation kept him before the public and the media, where he never felt very comfortable. The media, however, was too intrigued by the reluctant hero to be concerned by his need for peace or privacy.

When the American government asked Lindbergh to travel to Mexico in 1927 as a goodwill ambassador, his life took another unexpected turn. There he met and courted Anne Morrow, the daughter of American ambassador Dwight Morrow and Elizabeth Cutter Morrow. A shy, retiring woman with a love of books, Anne received a bachelor of arts degree from Smith College in 1928 and seemed the ideal companion for someone who preferred to avoid the public eye. Like her husband, however, Anne harbored a hidden adventurous nature. After they were married on May 27, 1929, Charles taught her to fly, and the couple spent long, happy hours in the sky, charting new routes for different airlines. By the following year, the Lindberghs' first child, Charles Augustus Jr., was born. Never happy with the continued media attention lavished on him, Lindbergh grew to resent the journalists who continued to hound him and his family. Although he tried at first to be civil, the news-papermen continued to ruthlessly intrude on their lives.

To escape, Lindbergh built a $50,000, twenty-room retreat off Amwell Road on 390 acres near what was then the rural community of Hopewell. On that fateful weekend at the end of February 1932, the family planned to stay for just a few nights in the country before returning to the estate of Anne's parents in Englewood. But Anne, pregnant with their second child, was anxious about young Charles, who had come down with a cold. They decided the baby was not well enough to travel and, as a result, planned to linger where they were for a few extra days. That unfortunate decision would shatter the tranquility of their lives worse than any media attention they had ever endured.

Five short years after his unprecedented flight, Lindbergh's luck ran out on the evening of March 1, when his twenty-month-old son was ruthlessly kidnapped from the family home. The horror began when young Charles's nurse, Betty Gow, returned to check on him at ten o'clock that night. She had stopped by the second-floor nursery two hours earlier to find the little boy sleeping peacefully in his crib, wearing the hand-sewn pajamas she had made for him. But now he was gone. Shocked, Gow told Lindbergh, who rapidly searched the property, then notified the newly formed New Jersey State Police. The police arrived with the press hot on their heels, eager to speculate about the fate of the Lindberghs' child. In the process, they probably trampled valuable evidence into the ground.

During a search of the property, police found a stepladder and some footprints several yards away near a wooded area. Although no fingerprints were discovered in the child's room, an envelope propped on the windowsill contained a single sheet of paper with a scrawled message in blue ink that read:

Dear Sir!

Have 50000$ redy with 2500$ in 20$ bills 1500$
in 10$ bills and 1000$ in 5$ bills. After 2–4 days
we will inform you were to deliver the Mony.
We warn you for making anyding public or for
notify the polise the child is in gute care.
Indication for all letters are singature and 3 holes.

Sketched in the bottom right corner of the page were two interlocking circles, each about one inch in diameter. The interior of the overlapping circles had been colored red, and three small holes were punched into the design.

Kidnapped. It was every parent's worst nightmare.

Although the fledgling state police had little experience in dealing with this type of crime, they quickly began assessing the physical evidence and questioning the Lindberghs and their staff regarding the evening's events. It soon became clear, however, that Lindbergh was not going to stand by quietly and wait for further instruction from the kidnappers—or from the police, for that matter. To make sure no one would prevent him from negotiating with the kidnappers, Lindbergh took immediate charge of the investigation. His status as a celebrity quickly ensured him of the cooperation he sought, even from the media, which he had viewed for so long as the enemy. He recruited help from newspapers and radio stations, which gladly cooperated in order to maintain access to the story. Before long, posters, magazine covers, and newspapers sported photos of the cherubic little boy, asking the public to help if they had any information about the crime. The Lindberghs even broadcast a plea to the kidnappers on NBC's radio station, promising to keep any contact confidential. A few days later, they received another poorly spelled note mailed from Brooklyn, stating that the child was safe and they would soon receive further instructions on where to deliver the money. While the police continued to question anyone and everyone who may have had contact with the family, Lindbergh accepted the assistance of a negotiator who claimed that he too had received correspondence from the kidnappers.

Dr. John Condon was a seventy-two-year-old retired school principal from the Bronx who had long been an admirer of Lindbergh. After reading about the kidnapping, Condon wrote a letter to his local newspaper, offering the kidnappers $1,000 of his own money as a supplement to the ransom, if they would communicate with him. The day after his letter was published, he called the Lindberghs to let them know he had received a response that allegedly came from the kidnappers. The note said that Condon was an acceptable liaison and contained a second letter to Lindbergh, which bore the same interlocking circles, punched with three small holes, at the bottom of the page. When they saw the same symbol that had appeared in the original ransom note, the anguished couple had no choice but to believe that Condon's correspondence with the kidnappers was authentic. The Lindberghs agreed that he should serve as a go-between, since the note also warned them not to contact the police and "not to set any trapp in any way."

In the weeks that followed, further correspondence—including a total of fifteen ransom notes—reportedly was exchanged between Condon and the kidnappers, and the ransom was increased to $70,000. As time dragged on, they threatened to increase the amount to $100,000 if the family did not soon comply with their demands. Further notes were delivered, offering directions on where and when to deliver payment. According to New Jersey State Police Museum archivist Mark Falzini, "Condon was driven to Woodlawn Cemetery on March 12, 1932, by his friend and bodyguard Al Reich, a former boxer." There he met for the first time the man who later became known as "Cemetery John." They talked across the cemetery fence, but when the cemetery guard came upon them, John hopped the fence and ran into a park across the street. Condon said he caught up to him there, and the two men sat on a park bench and talked for more than an hour. The kidnapper, who claimed not to be the ringleader, promised to send Condon a token to show that the baby was alive and well, then fled into the night. Apparently no one ever questioned how it was possible for a seventy-two-year-old man to catch a much younger man, who easily could have hidden himself in the shadows behind a building or even a tree.

A few days later, the pajamas that young Charles had been wearing when he was abducted appeared in Condon's mailbox. The sight of the child's clothes was sufficient proof for Lindbergh, who decided to pay the ransom. On April 2, the distraught father accompanied Condon to a cemetery in the Bronx that had been selected as the meeting place, where a shadowy figure just inside the gate demanded in a guttural German accent that Condon give him the money. When the stranger observed Lindbergh standing nearby, he grabbed the ransom, turned, and ran deeper into the grounds. Although Lindbergh had given Condon $70,000, only $50,000 in gold certificates was actually paid to the kidnappers. The certificates were paper money whose numbers had been recorded by the police. After the money was delivered, the former principal claimed to have received a note saying the child could be found on a small boat named the *Nellie,* about 150 miles away off the Massachusetts coast. Lindbergh immediately took to the air in the days that followed, but no such boat—and no baby—was ever found.

The Lindberghs were thoroughly discouraged, and their hopes were completely dashed about six weeks later, when the badly decomposed remains of a young child were found in the woods just several miles from their home. A truck driver named William Allen, who had entered a copse of trees about seventy-five feet from the road to relieve himself, was shocked to look down and see a tiny human form half buried in the ground close by where he was standing. After it was recovered, the baby's body was positively identified by his father as Charles Augustus Lindbergh Jr. and later autopsied. It was determined that the child had died from a blow to his head and that he had likely been dead for several months—probably since the very night of his kidnapping. Young Charles was later cremated at Trenton on May 13, 1932.

Although no more suspects had emerged in addition to "Cemetery John," the discovery of the child's body prompted authorities to once again question the Lindbergh staff. Violet Sharp, a maid who had previously seemed uncooperative during interviews, stated that she had been out on a date with a man named Ernie Brinkert on the night of March 1. Although police at first considered him a potential suspect because of his relationship with Sharp, Brinkert later proved to have an adequate alibi for his whereabouts during the kidnapping. In addition, his handwriting did not match any of the writing on the ransom notes. Speculation about Sharp's possible involvement in the crime remained alive for years, however, because the day after identifying Brinkert to the police, she committed suicide by drinking cyanide chloride from a measuring cup.

In the years that followed, a variety of law enforcement agencies, from the FBI to local police departments, worked to pursue leads on the Lindbergh case. According to www.charleslindbergh.com,

"In September, 1932, President Franklin D. Roosevelt state[d] in a meeting with J. Edgar Hoover that all work on the case be centralized in the Department of Justice." On October 19, 1933, the FBI was given jurisdiction in the kidnapping over all other agencies, and soon afterward the president also ordered the recall of all gold and gold certificates by the U.S. Treasury. Although this action was not directly related to the Lindbergh kidnapping, it decreased the number of bills in circulation and, as a result, increased the chances that authorities would be able to locate the ransom and the kidnappers. With the numbers of the bills released to all law enforcement agencies, the investigation intensified as additional rewards were offered and new leads surfaced. Unfortunately, each one proved to be false.

Although some of the money had surfaced just two days after the ransom had been paid, and it kept appearing from time to time, two years passed before tracking the gold certificates provided a real break in the case. While the police continued to investigate, the ransom notes were examined by handwriting experts, who concluded that they were all the work of one person. That person, they stated, was probably of German nationality but may have lived for a while in the United States. Authorities asked Arthur Koehler, a "wood expert" from the U.S. Forest Service, to inspect the ladder used in the kidnapping, and he determined that it had been built by someone with carpentry skills. In addition, Koehler believed that some of the wood had previously been part of the interior of a home—an opinion that would weigh heavily on the outcome of the kidnapper's trial, which was still a long way off.

It was September 18, 1934, when an assistant manager at the Corn Exchange Bank and Trust Company in New York alerted authorities that a teller had just received a $10 gold certificate from a customer. They soon learned that the bill had come from a neighborhood gas station, where the suspicious attendant had taken down the license plate number of the car. The vehicle's owner proved to be Bruno Richard Hauptmann of 1279 East 222nd Street in the

Bronx. After keeping the house under surveillance overnight, the police arrested Hauptmann at nine o'clock the following morning.

A German carpenter who had been living illegally in the United States for more than a decade, Hauptmann had another $20 gold certificate in his possession when he was arrested. After more than $14,000 worth of the ransom cash was unearthed the next day from his garage, he admitted that he had used the bills to make purchases around town. But according to Hauptmann, the money wasn't his. It belonged to another German immigrant, Isidor Fisch, a fur dealer who had left some of his property with the Hauptmanns before sailing the previous December to his native land. Unfortunately, the tale could not be corroborated, because Fisch died a few months later in Leipzig of tuberculosis. Hauptmann told the police that when he found the gold certificates in his friend's belongings, he decided to spend the money without telling anyone. Although she didn't know about the money, his wife, Anna, declared that her husband could not have been the kidnapper, because he had been at home with her on that fateful night. And Hauptmann continued to maintain his innocence despite the authorities' best efforts to obtain a confession.

In the weeks that followed, Hauptmann was fingerprinted and stood in line-ups. Handwriting samples that he provided were found to match the writing in the ransom notes. As investigators searched the suspect's house, they determined that wood in the ladder was the same as the wood flooring in his attic, and tool marks on it matched some of his carpentry tools. Another incriminating piece of evidence was the fact that Dr. Condon's telephone number and address were scrawled on a door frame inside a closet. Hauptmann had recently told family members and friends that after working for many years as a carpenter he had retired because some of his financial investments had finally paid off. That just didn't explain what he was doing with the ransom money.

With World War I still fresh in the public's mind, it was not surprising that many people were ready to believe the worst of this German immigrant, who not only had entered the country illegally, but also proved to have a criminal record in his homeland. Within hours of his arrest, press and police were clamoring for the death penalty for Hauptmann. After all, hadn't Lindbergh himself heard a voice with a German accent that night in the cemetery? Hauptmann was indicted for murder in Hunterdon County on October 8, 1934, and extradited from New York the following day. By New Year's Day, the residents of Flemington watched as their quiet town overflowed with hundreds of reporters and thousands of curious spectators, including celebrities such as Walter Winchell, Arthur Brisbane, Damon Runyon, and Jack Benny. When the trial started the next morning, it was presided over by Judge Thomas Trenchard, with the New Jersey attorney general David Wilentz serving as prosecutor. Hauptmann, escorted into the courtroom by a state trooper, was accompanied by his lawyer, Edward J. Reilly, known throughout the court system as the "Bull of Brooklyn."

In his opening statement, Wilentz called for the death penalty, as young Charles apparently had been killed when Hauptmann's ladder broke as he descended carrying the child. He then called Anne Lindbergh to the stand, who identified her son's pajamas and related what happened on the night of March 1. When Lindbergh was called to testify, he told the court that around nine o'clock, he had heard a strange noise from the kitchen, that sounded like an orange crate falling off a chair. He again identified Hauptmann's voice as the one he had heard in the cemetery. Although Condon had never previously identified the defendant as the man to whom he had paid the ransom, he didn't hesitate to tell the court that Hauptmann was the person he had met in the cemetery that night.

The defense responded by having Bruno Richard Hauptmann testify on his own behalf. In broken English, the suspect tried to describe his life in Germany and his ultimate illegal entry into the United States. He reiterated that the money in his garage belonged to Isidor Fisch. But during cross-examination, the prosecutor raised numerous questions about his finances, the missing board in the attic, and the discovery of Condon's telephone number in his closet—all of which Hauptmann found difficult to answer. His wife, Anna, then came to the stand and testified that her husband had been home with her that night. Other witnesses followed, including Swedish immigrant Elvert Carlson, who told the court that Hauptmann had been in his bakery on the night of the kidnapping, and August Van Henke, who testified that Hauptmann was walking his dog at the time of the kidnapping. But as Hauptmann watched in horror, Van Henke and almost all of the witnesses that followed were soon discredited by the prosecution. During the questioning, the defense attorney tried to cast suspicion on both the Lindbergh servants and Dr. Condon. He also chastised the state police for failing to properly identify evidence at the scene of the crime, including unknown footprints that were left unmeasured. In the end, however, his efforts were unsuccessful.

After presenting more than 150 witnesses, the opposing attorneys offered their summations. According to Hauptmann's attorney, the kidnapping had actually been masterminded by Condon, Fisch, and Sharp. He theorized that the crime had been an inside job—Sharp had stolen the child from his crib, then worked with Fisch and Condon to acquire the ransom. She committed suicide when she realized that the police were closing in. The ladder was just a fake clue planted outside the house to throw the authorities off the track. Wilentz followed with a five-hour summary of the evidence, calling Hauptmann the "public enemy number one of this world" and saying that there should be no mercy if the jury was convinced of his guilt.

The case against Hauptmann lasted for five weeks. Even though most of the evidence was circumstantial, it apparently was sufficient for the jury, which began deliberating on the morning of February 13 and reached a verdict less than twelve hours later. After jury foreman Charles Walton announced a few minutes later that the defendant, Bruno Richard Hauptmann, was guilty of murder in the first degree, Judge Trenchard asked Hauptmann to stand and pronounced the death sentence for his crime.

The trial was over.

The next day, Hauptmann told the press that he was innocent, even though he was advised that he could avoid the electric chair if he would only confess. But he was prepared to die rather than admit any guilt. Although his attorney filed an appeal, the Court of Errors and Appeals of the State of New Jersey upheld the verdict of the Lower Court on October 9, 1935. An appeal to the Supreme Court of the United States was denied on December 9. Hauptmann was originally scheduled to be electrocuted on January 17, 1936, but the governor of New Jersey unexpectedly granted him a thirty-day reprieve.

One reason for the delay had to do with Ellis Parker, the former chief detective of Burlington County, who, according to *New Jersey: A Guide to Its Present and Past,* "enjoyed a reputation as a suburban Sherlock Holmes." But Parker's efforts to aid the investigation involved "kidnapping Paul Wendel and obtaining by torture a confession of the Lindbergh murder," and when authorities realized what he had done, Hauptmann was resentenced on February 17 to be electrocuted during the week of March 30. On that date, the Pardon Court of the State of New Jersey denied Hauptmann's petition for clemency, and he was electrocuted on April 3, 1936, at 8:37 P.M. Parker was convicted the following year for his crimes; no explanation is given as to why Parker suspected Wendel, an innocent Trenton man.

Few incidents have captured the public imagination as much as the kidnapping of the Lindbergh baby. Even today debate continues to rage over many aspects of the case that became known as "the crime of the century." The shocking incident still enthralls the public because, some argue, the alleged kidnapper was simply a scapegoat, rushed to justice in large part because of his nationality. As Marc Mappen noted in *Jerseyana: The Underside of New Jersey History,* "It has also never been explained how a Bronx carpenter could have known so much about the layout and routine of the Lindbergh estate." Some question why Lindbergh rejected the request by the state police to use the newly invented polygraph (commonly known as a lie detector) system on his servants, even though he was assured it had at least a 90 percent accuracy rating.

At the same time, others argue that the evidence against the accused was more than sufficient. With all the publicity surrounding the Lindbergh kidnapping, it made sense for Hauptmann to keep the gold certificates hidden. Did he finally start spending them because he thought that a sufficient time had passed? Although it is unlikely that most of the questions will ever be resolved, alternative answers are still being offered to the question of who stole the Lindbergh baby. One current theory states that Lindbergh's sister-in-law, Elizabeth Morrow, killed her nephew in a jealous rage because Charles chose to marry Anne instead of her. Others speculate that the servants, in fact, were involved in a conspiracy with Dr. Condon to defraud the Lindberghs. After all, it wouldn't have been difficult to donate $1,000 as supplemental ransom if he knew it was going to be returned to him before long. Others place the blame on Lindbergh himself, suggesting that he created the kidnapping scenario after he killed the baby during rough play. If he was directly responsible for his son's death, that would be a good reason for him to assume control and dictate the course of the investigation.

Following the trial, the Lindberghs moved to England to escape the relentless media attention that had hounded them for so long. Although the couple went on to have five more children, they undoubtedly were always haunted by the memory of their firstborn, so ruthlessly taken from them. As the years passed, both Charles and Anne pursued a variety of interests in addition to flying. Charles, who later served as a fighter pilot during World War II, continued to experiment with new engineering designs, including one for an artificial heart, and Anne became an author and eventually wrote eleven books. Lindbergh died of cancer on August 26, 1974, and Anne died on February 7, 2001. Today we are familiar with Megan's Law and the Amber Alert, designed to assist law enforcement in capturing abducted children. Just three months after Charles Augustus Lindbergh Jr. was taken from his family, federal officials passed the Federal Kidnapping Act, more commonly known as the Lindbergh Law, which made kidnapping a federal offense if the victim was taken across state lines or if the mail service was used for ransom demands.

* * *

Although the Lindbergh case was the most acclaimed, it was not the only well-publicized crime that occurred in New Jersey during the Great Depression. According to *New Jersey: A Guide to Its Present and Past,* many residents of Andover were surprised to learn that their town was playing host to a notorious thief: "In October 1932, Arthur Barry, the cultured criminal whose hauls reputedly reached the figure of $2,000,000 was captured on a nearby farm where he had lived 15 months. The tip of an Andover shopkeeper from whom Barry had purchased New York newspapers led to the arrest of the dapper, mustached second-story man who had fled to Andover after escaping from Auburn Prison in New York." But Barry's arrest paled in comparison with another criminal case that soon rose to national prominence. This one had unfolded with all the scandalous ingredients of adultery, intrigue, and murder.

In 1935, Newark resident Mary Frances Creighton was tried and convicted along with her lover, Everett Appelgate, of poisoning Everett's wife, Ada. Creighton, who had been acquitted a decade earlier of killing several family members, apparently wanted to marry Appelgate and wasn't about to let the presence of a wife stand in her way. Neither did she seem to care that Appelgate was carrying on a torrid affair with her fifteen-year-old daughter at the same time he was sleeping with her. The following year, Creighton was transferred to Sing Sing Prison and was one of only a handful of women ever to be executed in the electric chair.

Three short years later, Burlington County residents lived in fear of a shotgun-wielding killer who preyed on couples who visited the isolated peninsula of Duck Island, which was well known as a "lover's lane." The "Duck Island Killer," as he was dubbed by the media, also robbed and killed people in nearby Pennsylvania towns. His New Jersey victims included Trenton residents Vincenzo "Jim" Tonzillo and Mary Myatovich, as well as Louis Kovacs and Carolina Morconi. It wasn't until 1941 that authorities finally captured Clarence Hill of Hamilton Township, a married laborer who confessed to the crimes. Although the prosecutor sought the death penalty, the jury recommended mercy, and Hill spent less than twenty years behind bars. When he was paroled in 1964, he disappeared quietly into civilian life. The man who had committed what was then the worst string of murders in Mercer County history died of natural causes on July 9, 1973.

In the years that followed Hill's rampage, New Jersey residents periodically picked up their morning newspapers to read accounts of other dramatic crimes. There was twenty-eight-year-old Howard Unruh, a World War II veteran living in Camden, whose paranoia, perhaps induced by post-traumatic stress disorder, led him to pick up a gun on September 5, 1949, and start shooting everyone in sight—including a three-year-old neighbor. Eight years later, a twenty-three-year-old sociopath named Edgar Herbert Smith was convicted of murdering Victoria Zielinski, a fifteen-year-old high school student in Mahwah. While on death row, Smith wrote a book about his trial, titled *Brief against Death,* which attracted the attention of noted author William F. Buckley. With Buckley as his champion against the judicial system, which Smith claimed had railroaded him into prison, the smooth-talking inmate successfully appealed his sentence. But despite his protests of innocence, Smith, who eventually wrote two more books about his arrest and trial, assaulted and murdered another woman in 1976 after he was released. This crime returned him to prison for the remainder of his days.

In 1966, Paterson native Rubin "Hurricane" Carter, who had learned to box in prison, was arrested and charged with the murder of three people. His conviction was overturned almost twenty years later, because a Federal District Court judge ruled that racial overtones in the prosecutor's closing remarks had improperly influenced the jury.

Then there was the puzzling disappearance in 1971 of an upstanding Westfield man—a mystery that became even more baffling with the discovery of the bodies of his family.

CHAPTER 3
The Fugitive

✳ ✳ ✳

In his version of the story, he was saving their souls by removing them from the temptations of the world. Yet no one else seemed to appreciate the claims of mercy behind John List's actions when he brutally killed every member of his family and then disappeared, managing afterward to "hide in plain sight" for almost twenty years.

Westfield is a small, prosperous community of about 30,000 people that traces its roots to the mid-seventeenth century, when English colonists purchased the land from the Lenni-Lenape. Up until 1971, it was perhaps best known as the home of Charles Addams, the cartoonist whose winsomely creepy characters became the inspiration for the popular television show titled *The Addams Family*. That year, however, the upper-income Union County community became infamous as the town where forty-six-year-old John List murdered his entire family.

Westfield residents were stunned when the bodies of List's forty-five-year-old wife, Helen; their three children, sixteen-year-old

Patty, fifteen-year-old John Jr., and thirteen-year-old Frederick; and List's eighty-five-year-old widowed mother, Alma, were discovered in Breeze Knoll, the abandoned family home on Hillside Avenue, just weeks before Christmas. The elegant nineteen-room mansion had originally been built at the turn of the twentieth century by millionaire John S. A. Wittke for his sister Etta and was still considered a local status symbol in the 1970s. The Lists, who had been unable to establish many ties to the community, soon became known by just about every household in Westfield as well as throughout the United States.

Although the house remained impressive looking from the outside, the Lists were never able to restore Breeze Knoll to its former glory as they had initially planned. Their new home was supposed to show the world that they had finally "arrived." But during the years they lived there, the interior remained almost completely devoid of the comforts that make a house a home. Many of the rooms, including a cavernous second-floor ballroom, were sparsely decorated, because the family simply could not afford to buy furniture. The Lists had almost bankrupted themselves just by purchasing the house when they moved there in the mid-1960s from Bay City, Michigan. The family moved east after List accepted a job as vice president and comptroller at the First National Bank in Jersey City. He decided to settle in Westfield after learning there was a good Lutheran school situated in the town. List's religion had been a focal point of his life since childhood, and he was determined to instill those same values in his children.

At the time, the average home in Westfield sold in the $20,000 to $30,000 range. But when the realtor showed them the Wittke mansion, John and Helen decided they had to have it—even though the price tag was $50,000. In the end, the only way they could afford it at all was when Alma agreed to sell her Bay City home and move into an apartment on the third floor of the new house, which had been set aside for her use. Most of the neighbors didn't know anything about the personal lives of the List family, let alone the condition of the house. Few outsiders ever crossed the threshold, because from the first, the Lists proved to be less than welcoming to most of their neighbors. Alma was occasionally willing to socialize, and the children made tentative efforts to establish friendships, but John and Helen preferred to keep to themselves. Although the reason for their behavior may have had a more sinister motive, it could have been fueled by nothing more than embarrassment. Like their lives, the rambling white house had appeared to be perfect—on the outside.

During the investigation that followed the murders, authorities learned something that proved even more shocking than the fact that the Lists were living beyond their means. They soon discovered that John List had apparently spent months planning his heinous crime before disappearing into the night. A solitary man, List preferred not to spend time with anyone besides his family and the congregation of the Redeemer Evangelical Lutheran Church, which he faithfully attended each week. But he lived in an upper-income neighborhood and caught the train into work every day, just like most local residents. Most people figured that his job as an accountant had to be providing the family with a sufficient income. It was undoubtedly troubling for many Westfield residents to think that List, who appeared no different than anyone else in the upscale suburban community, was capable of such a horrible crime.

Although List's actions at first seemed completely out of character, authorities quickly discovered that the middle-aged accountant felt he had adequate reasons for committing mass murder. He apparently had convinced himself that the 1970s were sinful times that undermined all family values. During the Age of Aquarius, as the period was sometimes known, America was exploding with protestors, marching against U.S. involvement in Vietnam and for causes such as minority groups' and women's rights. A maniacal young man named Charles Manson had gathered a cult around him to commit crimes that shocked the nation, including the murder of actress Sharon Tate. Most Westfield residents probably just shook their heads over such incidents and counted themselves grateful that horrific crimes like the Tate murder didn't happen in their town. In all likelihood, the unsuspecting members of the List family probably felt much the same way before they were struck down. While they undoubtedly were looking forward to the end-of-the-year holidays, just like their friends and neighbors, their father was quietly calculating their deaths with the same cold logic he would have used to solve any other troublesome equation.

When the bodies of the List family were discovered, the question on everyone's lips was, Why? What had motivated a seemingly happily married, college-educated man to suddenly kill his entire family? A World War II Army veteran who had achieved the rank of lieutenant, he later earned a master's degree in accounting. Some psychologists would argue that List, like other murderers before him, grew up in a repressed environment that stifled him emotionally. His father was distant, and his mother compensated by being overprotective. He seemed to have difficulty coping with people and frequently lost his job as a result. Although no one knows exactly when the seed for List's plan was planted, it may have first taken root two years earlier, when his wife, Helen, informed him that she had been hiding a secret from him for most of their marriage. She confessed that she had contracted syphilis, a sexually transmitted disease, from her first husband, Marvin, who had been killed during World War II. As her symptoms worsened, so did her relationship with her husband.

In *Righteous Carnage: The List Murders,* authors Timothy B. Benford and James P. Johnson noted that List had felt no small degree of guilt over his attraction to Helen Morris Taylor, whom he had met while in the Army. That guilt was compounded after they had sex before marriage and she became pregnant with their first child. List had initially been willing to ignore the fact that she had been raised as a Southern Methodist and showed little interest in adopting the Lutheran faith. Authorities later learned that List attributed some of the difficulties in the marriage to the fact that

Helen had not been Lutheran and, as years passed, showed little respect for his faith.

Helen grew to resent List's close ties to his mother and began to drink heavily, while he was unsympathetic about her progressively degenerating health. Not long after Helen made the startling announcement about her condition, both she and their daughter, Patty, stopped going to church. List apparently believed the situation threatened not only his authority as head of the household, but their immortal souls as well. Patty, who was active in the local community theater group, also was believed to have been dabbling in the occult, like many teenagers of the period—an interest that undoubtedly shocked her churchgoing father.

By 1971, List had lost his job as the bank vice president and had spiraled downward in a series of lesser-paying positions. In the year preceding the murders, he had brought home an income of less than $5,000. The mansion was remortgaged twice, and the family was falling behind in the payments. Then List lost his job again and was too proud to inform his family that they would soon have to give up their elegant house in the prestigious neighborhood. While he kept borrowing money for the mortgage and utilities from his mother, he eventually ran through her $200,000 in savings. As months passed and the family got further behind on the bills, he continued to leave the house in the morning as though he were going to work, heading to the trains along with countless other local commuters.

For a while, he spent his days wandering the platforms or the city streets, unwilling to seek unemployment compensation or any other type of public assistance that would have kept his family financially afloat. As Benford and Johnson explained, "John Emil List learned from his father's example that to go on welfare was to admit that you were not a man." This idea had been strongly reinforced on a daily basis during the Depression, as young John watched his father go from owning a business to peddling food from his car in order to support his family.

As he began to assess his situation, List soon began to focus more attention on those closest to him. He didn't much like what he saw. With his home life collapsing, List believed there was only one way he could "save" the people he loved: He had to kill them while they were still Christians to be sure that they would reach heaven in the next life. He couldn't kill himself afterward, however, since suicide was considered a sin. So his punishment would be to live with the guilt of his actions. He was sure that God would forgive him when he died so that he would someday be reunited with his family.

In October 1971, he applied for a gun permit and soon brought a .9-millimeter automatic and a .22-caliber pistol into the house, ostensibly for home protection. Because he believed he was killing his family for a higher purpose, List didn't feel that he should be subject to any human authority, who probably would not understand his actions. As a result, he began to plan his escape. While other local residents commuted to their offices in Philadelphia and neighboring towns, List began to take train trips to Denver, Colorado, and Michigan. There, in his home state, he laid the foundation for another identity. That's when his alter ego, Robert Clark, was born.

In November, he had the mail and milk deliveries stopped. Unknown to the rest of the family, List had previously told school authorities that the children would be missing classes for a while because they were going to visit his wife's sick mother in North Carolina. But Patty had her suspicions. Previous discussions around the dinner table, with her father probing the children about their own deaths, began to take their toll. Anxious and fearful, she informed her high school drama coach that her father planned to murder the family—an announcement that unfortunately was not taken seriously. On the wintry morning of November 9, after the children had left for school, List came downstairs to breakfast and shot his wife in the back of the head while she sat at the kitchen table. When he was finished, he climbed to his mother's third-floor apartment and shot her point-blank in the face. Since she was too heavy to carry downstairs, List shoved her body into a storage area and, after covering her face with a kitchen towel, left her where she lay.

That afternoon, he picked up Patty at school and killed her when they arrived home. He later shot Frederick, his younger son, when he got home from school, then dragged his body upstairs and laid him alongside his mother and sister in the empty second-floor ballroom of the house. As they investigated, authorities came to believe that John Jr. may have suspected something was wrong when he arrived home from his after-school job. He may have tried to escape, because he was—unlike the others—shot more than once by his father. Once everything had been arranged to his satisfaction, List cleaned up the house, ate dinner, and went to bed. He disappeared the next morning, after turning on the intercom, which began to softly play churchlike music through the house.

After a few weeks, the neighbors became concerned by the lack of activity at the List home. Lights that had been left on during the day—something they knew the frugal family would never do—began to flicker out, leaving the house in constant darkness. When authorities finally entered the abandoned house, it wasn't hard to figure out what had happened, although more than a month had passed since the crimes occurred. List quickly became the only suspect after the police discovered the guns and ammunition used to kill his family in a room that had previously served as a home office. Authorities later learned that the fugitive had read a number of books on committing murder and, according to www.crimelibrary.com, was heard to comment that it would be very easy for an accountant who had access to Social Security numbers and other personal information to establish a new identity. Most damning was the three-page letter List left for Eugene A. Rehwinkel, the pastor of his church, admitting his actions and detailing his crimes. But List himself was nowhere to be found. He had vanished so completely that it seemed as though he, in fact, had already gone to join his family in the afterlife.

In actuality, he had moved to Golden, a suburb of Denver, where he worked for a time as a night cook in a Holiday Inn. Robert Clark, as he was now known, lived a solitary life, sharing only a few details about himself with Bob Wetmore, who also worked the night shift in the hotel kitchen. After a while, List moved on to better jobs that allowed him to settle in more comfortable surroundings. He bought a car and began attending the local Lutheran church, where he was considered a model parishioner. There, in 1977, he met and eventually married Delores Miller, an attractive woman who shared his standards and beliefs.

While the investigation foundered, the local newspapers occasionally ran stories about List's mysterious disappearance and the tragedy. In the years that followed, the police continued to investigate and tried a variety of methods of locating List, including the distribution of an age-progressed sketch of the fugitive. None of the avenues they explored produced any results, however. In 1985, Detective Jeffrey Paul Hummel was assigned to review the file and decided to try a new approach to resolving the fourteen-year-old case. Hummel, personally appalled by the crime, consulted psychic Elizabeth Lerner of Ocean County, knowing she had previously assisted other police departments on their investigations with some success. After handling photographs of the crime scene for several hours, the psychic provided him with information about List and his movements since he had left New Jersey—information that ultimately proved for the most part to be correct. According to Lerner, List was in fact alive and had left the area either by bus or train, despite the fact that his 1963 Chevrolet Impala had been discovered in the long-distance parking lot of the Kennedy International Airport. She said that there was a new woman in his life, and authorities later discovered that he had married Miller in Denver. List, the psychic added, had fled southwest but would probably be discovered living in Florida or Virginia. Authorities later learned that List had initially fled to Colorado, but he was eventually arrested in Virginia.

Unfortunately, Hummel was eventually transferred to a narcotics strike force, which meant searching for John List was no longer his first responsibility. But as often happens to dedicated police officers, the crime continued to haunt him—and others, as well. In 1987, the Newark office of the FBI asked the Special Projects Section of the FBI Laboratory to use new computer technology to create age-enhanced photographs of John List. When the photographs were released in the national media, a woman recognized him as Robert Clark, who was then her neighbor. But rather than contact the authorities, she chose to inform Clark's wife about the photographs in a supermarket tabloid, which spurred List to run again.

This information never reached New Jersey authorities, and Hummel asked Capt. Frank Marranca, head of the Major Crimes Unit in Elizabeth, if he would consider exploring another unusual avenue to try to locate the longtime fugitive. Hummel proposed that the department take advantage of a new television show called *America's Most Wanted,* which assisted the police in locating criminals on the run by profiling cases from different states each week. Although the program usually focused on more recent crimes, the List case piqued the interest of its producers. Marranca gave Hummel's suggestion his seal of approval, and in the end, his decision proved to be a good one. The show ultimately resolved the eighteen-year-old mystery of what had happened to John List.

Modern technology has repeatedly proved itself useful to law enforcement. Although DNA and other forensic methods were still in their infancy in 1989, *America's Most Wanted* used the artistic talents of Frank Bender to create a forensic sculpture of List. Bender's work in the field had previously helped authorities capture other fugitives, as well as accurately identify decomposed bodies. After thoroughly researching his subject and consulting a forensic psychologist, Bender developed his own psychological profile of John List. He studied photographs of List's parents and finally created a clay bust of List, which showed how he might look after almost twenty years. Bender provided his subject with a receding hairline, a sagging jaw, and a pair of heavy, dark-framed glasses. Although the Westfield police were not optimistic after so many years, Bender's handiwork quickly generated a response when the show aired.

Ironically enough, John List—who was living in Virginia at the time—later admitted that he was a fan of the show that led to his capture. But he missed most of the episode that chronicled his story the night it aired. He did see enough to decide that he would not run again if the authorities came calling, which they did after a neighbor recognized List and anonymously contacted the FBI. According to the woman, the sculpture shown on *America's Most Wanted* bore a striking likeness to the man she knew as Robert Clark.

Federal agents arrived at the fugitive's home on June 1, where they met Mrs. Clark. After the FBI showed her a picture of John List, she brought out her wedding photo and discovered, much to her dismay, that she was standing next to the same man. When Mrs. Clark said her husband was at work, several agents went to Clark's office. Although Clark was cooperative when he was first approached, he vehemently denied that his true identity was that of John Emil List. Repeatedly declaring that his name was Robert Clark, the sixty-two-year-old suspect was brought to the local FBI headquarters for fingerprinting. There the agents discovered that they had in fact captured the murderer who had eluded authorities for almost two decades. Initially held without bail, List pleaded not guilty to the murder of his family during his arraignment, where bail was set at $1 million. Following an extradition hearing, he soon found himself back in New Jersey for the first time in eighteen years.

Elijah Miller, List's court-appointed defense attorney, requested a change of venue for the trial because of all the publicity generated by List's capture. He also tried to suppress the confession that List had left for his pastor, but because he had to do this in the name of John List, not Robert Peter Clark, he stopped insisting that the state prove that Clark and List were the same man. Miller's defense opened with the fact that List had indeed murdered his family on November 9, 1971, but the murders happened because he had an obsessive-compulsive personality disorder and was ill-equipped to function in the face of the emotional and financial difficulties that had threatened to overwhelm him. A psychiatrist called in to testify for the defense said that List lost control when he started killing, but he truly believed that his actions had saved the souls of his family, who were being corrupted by life in a godless world.

The prosecutor, Eleanor Clark, told the court that far from being a God-fearing man, John List was selfish, cruel, and deliberate in his plans to rid himself of his family and start a new, unencumbered life. But like any good accountant, she said, he felt compelled to balance the books before he closed the account. List had knowingly and willfully killed his family—a statement that was fully supported by the autopsies, fingerprints, ballistics reports, and even his own words. In fact, the prosecutor put a psychiatrist on the stand who said that John List's only disorder was depression stemming from a midlife crisis. Throughout the trial, the defendant remained calm and apparently unmoved by the evidence against him.

The trial on five counts of murder in the first degree lasted seven days, and on April 12, 1990, List was found guilty on all counts. In the end, List's allegedly spiritual motivation, coupled with the story of how his first wife, Helen, had kept her syphilis secret from him for so many years, failed to elicit the hoped-for sympathy from the jury. His sentence was five consecutive life terms, which meant that he would never be released from prison. Consecutive sentences are served one after the other, while concurrent terms are served at the same time.

Unlike other murderers, he did not become just another number in the crowd. In March 2002, Connie Chung interviewed John List for ABC's evening magazine show *Downtown.* For the first time in thirty years, despite the passage of time, List detailed some of the events that had occurred on that fateful November day. He related that he had shot his wife from behind while she ate toast at the kitchen table. After removing her body and cleaning up the blood, he sat down at the table to eat his lunch. He then described how shooting his mother fulfilled his late father's request to take care of her and make sure she didn't suffer by being left alone in this world. List was almost eighty when he was interviewed by Chung and seemed to feel absolutely no remorse for what he had done. According to www.crimelibrary.com, at one point, he even asked Chung if it weren't possible that his actions could be interpreted as something besides cold-blooded murder.

As for the elegant List mansion, it mysteriously burned down on August 30, 1972, less than a year after the murders. Some thought the blaze may have been caused accidentally by teens, who held parties at the site; others believed it may have been set by a professional arsonist. The property was later auctioned by First Federal Savings, the primary mortgage holder, and was purchased for $36,100 by Kurt C. Bauer, editor and publisher of the *News-Record,* a weekly Rahway newspaper. According to Benford and Johnson, Bauer had a "massive Georgian brick colonial" built on the property. Sadly, the fire also had destroyed the one object in the home that could have resolved the List family's money problems and perhaps saved the lives of five innocent people. According to an article in the February 17, 2001, *Westfield Leader,* "The glass ceiling in the empty ball room was a signed Tiffany original. That alone would likely have paid off all of John List's debts." At the time, the estimated value of such a treasure was more than $100,000. List is currently serving his sentences at the New Jersey State Prison in Trenton, where he divides his time between working as an accountant and writing his own book about the tragedy.

* * *

Like most states, New Jersey had its share of violent racial confrontations during the 1960s and 1970s. One crime that occurred during the turmoil remains open, and the convicted criminal is still at large. The year was 1973. Then, the young woman was known as

Joanne Chesimard, a member of the Black Liberation Army, a revolutionary group that promoted the overthrow of the U.S. government. Convicted of murdering New Jersey state trooper Werner Foerster during a routine traffic stop that erupted into a gun battle, Chesimard was tried and sentenced in 1977 to life in the Edna Mahan Correctional Facility for Women in Hunterdon County. Two years later, she escaped from the prison, and in 1986, she found political asylum in Cuba, where she reportedly still resides under the name of Assata Shakur. But in New Jersey, she will always be known as Joanne Chesimard—the woman who literally got away with murder, with a $1 million federal bounty offered for her capture.

In the midst of the social upheaval that occurred at that time, another criminal surfaced whose actions boggled the minds of both law enforcement authorities and psychologists who studied pathological behavior. And though more than thirty years have passed since he was caught and convicted for his crimes, the case of Joseph Kallinger remains both disturbing and intriguing.

CHAPTER 4
The Shoemaker and His Children

* * *

Most father-son outings are innocent enough: maybe a little fishing, a ball game, or even a trip to the mountains for some skiing. Little did a Leonia family know that when two strangers invaded their home one winter day and committed murder, it was one man's perverted idea of spending quality time with his son.

Murder, sexual assault, and robbery were just some of the more serious charges laid against Philadelphia native Joseph Kallinger after he was captured by authorities at his home on January 17, 1976. But to this day, the man behind a seven-week-long, tri-state crime spree throughout the Delaware Valley remains an enigma that is frequently debated but has not yet been solved by psychologists, psychiatrists, and other students of aberrant behavior.

Who was Joseph Kallinger? On the surface, he was a family man who earned his living as a shoemaker. Beneath the surface was another story entirely. Although the neighbors may have dismissed him as a little strange, it is unlikely that anyone who lived on East Sterner Street in the working-class neighborhood of Philadelphia's Kensington district in the early 1970s would have believed that the burly cobbler would eventually become the target of a massive police manhunt throughout Pennsylvania, New York, and New Jersey. What most of them didn't know was that the façade of normalcy, which had shielded Kallinger up until that time, was rapidly disintegrating. Whatever the reason, the shoemaker, like Dr. Henry Jekyll, would soon present a different face to the world, one that he seemed to be able to summon at will.

Although he led a seemingly unremarkable life for almost forty years, Kallinger later claimed that he had been tormented by voices and hallucinations since childhood. These supernatural influences, he said, were responsible for making him commit robbery and murder. After he was caught, however, he apparently realized that neither God nor the devil were subject to earthly law. That was when Kallinger found someone a little closer to home to blame for his more serious crimes—his twelve-year-old son, Michael.

According to Kallinger, he would have been content to just rob people as he and Michael rode the bus out of Philadelphia into the Pennsylvania countryside and into New Jersey. It was Michael, he said, who wanted more. It was Michael, he said, who demanded that they kill someone. Although the slight, blond-haired boy was never charged in any of the crimes that the two allegedly committed, he was easily identified by witnesses as having been present during a number of home invasions and actively participating in the robberies. Yet authorities knew he was an unlikely mastermind and did not take Kallinger's claims seriously. At the same time, they undoubtedly wondered what prompted the boy to accompany his father on these bizarre outings.

In all likelihood, Michael was probably too intimidated by Kallinger to refuse—especially after his elder brother, fourteen-year-old Joseph Jr., became one of their father's first victims. Joseph Kallinger was physically a bear of a man, whose upper body had been strengthened by years of hard work. Before his crime spree, he reportedly assaulted not only his first wife and later his second, but his children as well. That's probably why Michael decided it was better to do as he was told, since he knew the authorities couldn't hurt him anywhere nearly as bad as his father had done over the years. So when Kallinger decreed that his son accompany him on his travels, Michael obeyed.

After the shoemaker was arrested, medical experts called in by the authorities vigorously debated his actions: Was Kallinger's behavior the result of his own allegedly abusive past? Or was he yet another sociopath who had decided that the world at large should pay for the inequities he had suffered in life? Although Kallinger later asserted that other beings in addition to Michael were responsible for his actions, it is clear that at some point he chose to begin robbing and assaulting unsuspecting homeowners.

According to an October 30, 1983 article in the *Boston Globe,* Kallinger was born on December 11, 1936, "conceived during a brief affair between a twenty-one-year-old woman who was separated from her husband and a man who was married to someone else. She kept her baby for a month, then gave him up to a boarding home in Philadelphia; later he was sent to an orphanage." Kallinger was not quite two years old when he was adopted by Austrian immigrants Stephen and Anna Kallinger, who operated a flourishing shoe repair business attached to their red brick row home in the Kensington section of Philadelphia. Little is known about the couple. The bulk of information, which has since become accepted as fact, was provided by Kallinger to author Flora Rheta Schreiber, who demonized the couple in her book *The Shoemaker: Anatomy of a Psychotic.*

Kallinger said his adoptive parents brutally mistreated him as a child. A lonely boy, by the time he was seven, Kallinger was allegedly required to spend every day after school and all day Saturdays repairing shoes. He claimed to have been flogged with a whip, beaten with a hammer, and frequently threatened with banishment to the orphanage from which he had been adopted. He told Schreiber that the only reason he, in fact, had been adopted by the Kallingers was because they wanted free labor to help run their business. Kallinger also claimed that his adoptive parents repeatedly threatened to have him emasculated, a topic that he began to obsess over as a boy. Then, when he turned eight, Kallinger said he was sexually assaulted by a gang of older boys, who threatened him with a knife. He told Schreiber that this incident so traumatized him that he began to associate sex and violence in his mind. As he got older, he said, he would masturbate while clutching a knife in one hand.

To escape his allegedly abusive home life, Kallinger married at seventeen and had two children with Hilda, his first wife. They were divorced within three years, however, after his mistreated wife left him for another man. The following year, Kallinger was hospitalized for a brain lesion, but his real ailment proved to be a psychopathological nervous disorder. Despite his condition, Kallinger married again in April 1958 and had five children with his second wife, Elizabeth. Although an aborted suicide attempt sent him briefly to a state hospital in 1959, Kallinger soon returned home and began a lucrative new sideline to his shoemaking business—arson. He burned his own home in order to claim a $1,600 fire insurance settlement. He later set fire to the family's next home on four separate occasions between 1963 and 1967.

His new interest apparently kindled more than just the furnishings. Before long, he realized he could extend his criminal activities into other areas.

By 1972, the Kallingers had six children at home, including two from his first marriage. Tensions apparently ran high in the crowded row home, because three of his children, including Joe Jr., complained that year to the police that they were being abused by their father. Both Kallinger and Elizabeth denied the charges when they were contacted, but after the children were examined by a doctor, authorities arrested the shoemaker on three counts of abuse. Although a court-ordered examination revealed that Kallinger had a number of emotional and psychological problems, he was ultimately found intelligent enough and mentally fit to stand trial. Convicted on all charges, his sentence was the seven months he had already served behind bars while awaiting trial.

His return soon cast a pall over the household, which had enjoyed a brief stint of peace while Kallinger was imprisoned. Then, in February 1973, authorities were surprised when the three Kallinger children appeared before a judge and declared that they had lied about their father's abuse. Although the police feared that the children had been coerced by their parents into changing their stories, the judge had no alternative but to clear Kallinger's record following their testimony. Kallinger later told authorities that he had asked the children to clear his name in order not to ruin his business. Joe Jr. was declared emotionally disturbed by social workers, who determined that he should be sent to a Bucks County reformatory to receive counseling. Yet despite their findings, the boy was allowed weekend passes to return to Philadelphia. Two months after Joe Jr. was released from custody in May 1974, his father took out a $45,000 life insurance policy on him and another son. Kallinger claimed that the boys were such troublemakers that he expected something bad to happen to either one or both of them.

Later that same July, Joe Jr. went missing. In August, his body was found in the sub-basement of a building at Ninth and Market streets that was scheduled for demolition.

Although the authorities could not prove murder, they refused to believe Kallinger's story that the boy was probably responsible for his own death. And just as he apparently did with the fires, Kallinger—recognizing the potential for further profit—continued his pattern of abuse against his other children after Joe Jr. died. That September, another bruised and bloodied son was discovered wandering around the city of Camden. When the Philadelphia police tried to investigate on the child's behalf, Kallinger successfully filed a lawsuit against them for harassment.

Late that fall, Kallinger apparently was so encouraged by his ability to outwit the law that he began to take Michael on "field trips" to New Jersey. On November 22, 1974, they burglarized a house in Lindenwold, and Kallinger sexually assaulted a woman after they invaded another different home in the same town later that day. Less than two months later, Kallinger committed another sexual assault on a woman in Dumont. His appetite increasing with each attack, Kallinger forced three women to perform oral sex on him during another home invasion, and in another instance, he attempted to rape one of his victims. In one Pennsylvania home, he demanded that the four women there strip off their clothes while he and Michael robbed the house. During the incident, he wounded one woman with a knife, before escaping with $20,000 worth of goods.

On January 8, 1975, the bus dropped off Kallinger and Michael in the quiet town of Leonia. The small upscale community of less than 10,000 people, located just miles away from New York, was incorporated in 1894 and has been home to a number of notables, including actor Alan Alda and author Robert Ludlum. There the Kallingers wandered the neighborhoods, searching for likely targets. Although a number of people later told police they noticed the strange pair, no one paid very much attention to their movements. Before long, father and son arrived at 124 Glenwood Avenue, the comfortable suburban home of Edwinna and DeWitt Romaine. At that time, the Romaines were in the midst of a family crisis that had brought their oldest daughter, Didi Wiseman, home to help out. DeWitt had suffered a heart attack just a few weeks before Christmas and was still hospitalized. Edwinna had to divide her time between caring for her ninety-year-old bedridden grandmother, who lived with them, and daily visits to check on her husband. Her twin daughters, Randi and Retta, still lived at home, but Edwinna was delighted to have Didi on hand as well, especially since she brought along her four-year-old son.

That cold winter day, Didi was looking after her grandmother while Edwinna and the twins were at the hospital. Didi later told authorities that although she had noticed the dark-haired man and blond boy—later identified as Kallinger and his son Michael—

walking near the house earlier that day, she never expected to find them on her doorstep later that afternoon after everyone had left. When she responded to that fateful knock at the door, she found it difficult to believe that the man was a John Hancock insurance salesman, as he claimed. He smelled funny and certainly wasn't dressed in appropriate business clothing. And she had never heard of a salesman bringing a child along on the job. Before she could act on her instincts, however, the man forced his way into the house, followed by the silent boy.

Once inside, the boy began to ransack the house while the man forced Didi and her son upstairs. After ordering them to disrobe, he tied them up and helped his accomplice search the bedrooms for any valuables. The young mother and her child were terrified by the strange pair, who vandalized the house as they searched for things to steal. But what frightened Didi more was the fact that before long, more victims would be caught by the intruders. Sure enough, when Randi returned from the hospital a while later, she was surprised to discover that the front door was locked. After she rang the doorbell, she was horrified to be greeted by a total stranger instead of her sister or nephew.

The smiling man, who pulled her inside and forced her up the stairs, explained that he was there to rob the house. After Randi showed him where she kept her cash, the man demanded that she remove her clothing. Randi refused—until he pulled out a knife. When the intruder demanded to know who else was coming home, Randi said that the Romaines were expecting a large number of guests. But the stranger didn't seem to care; his attention was focused on Randi. To avoid being raped, she told the man she was menstruating, and her quick thinking saved her from an assault. The man tied and gagged her while the silent boy looked on; then they continued to search the house. She could only hope that her sister and nephew would be safe from the intruders.

Before she could even think about attempting to escape, Randi was dismayed to hear the doorbell ring once again.

When Edwinna and her daughter Retta, accompanied by Retta's boyfriend, Frank Welby, returned from the hospital, they were completely unprepared for the nightmare that awaited them inside. Like Randi, they were greeted at the door by the intruder, but this time he was holding a gun. As they were ordered inside, Edwinna began to hyperventilate, and her loved ones feared that she would suffer a heart attack like her husband. Not that it mattered to the stranger. He ordered the women to lie facedown on the living room floor near the television, and he told Welby to lie by the fireplace. After stripping them all of their jewelry, he tied their feet together with cords he had cut from household appliances. Once they were secured, the two intruders went back to searching the house. Afraid of what would happen if the man and boy returned, Edwinna and Retta began to struggle quietly with their bonds. Slowly working their hands free, the two women waited to seize an opportunity to escape. But before they could move, the Romaines heard the front doorbell ring again, and yet another victim was ushered into the scene.

Maria Fasching, a nurse from the hospital, had arrived for a visit with the twins. The three young women had gone to high school together and remained friends through the years. She was not the least bit intimidated by the man with the gun, and the others could hear her fearlessly ordering him to leave. The family had gone through too much already, she told him. But the stranger soon forced her to lie facedown in the living room next to Welby, who moments later was rapidly propelled down the basement steps. In all likelihood, the strangers probably saw Retta's six-foot-three boyfriend as much more of a threat than the women. Welby was gagged with a handkerchief and his head was covered with adhesive tape. He later told authorities that he thought he heard Maria Fasching being escorted into another basement room a few minutes later. Deafened by the furnace blower, he could not be sure whether he actually heard any screaming. Though Welby may not have been able to hear her, everyone else listened horror-stricken to the nurse's cries and her final chilling words: "I'm drowning!" They later found out that she, in fact, had drowned in her own blood after the stranger cut her throat.

Afraid for her life and those of her loved ones, Edwinna began to scream. At that point, she undoubtedly believed that the intruders were going to kill them all. With superhuman effort, she hobbled out of the house and into the street, still screaming at the top of her lungs. According to www.crimelibrary.com, a concerned neighbor, Lucy Bevacqua, afraid that Edwinna was having a nervous breakdown because of her husband's condition, soon called the police. But when the officers responded to the Romaine home that afternoon, they found a much more serious situation than simply a distraught homemaker.

As Retta hid under the couch, she heard the boy alert his companion that her mother had escaped. The intruders bolted out the back door as the officers came through the front door and assisted the family. After authorities converged on the scene, they later learned that a woman who was out walking her dog in a nearby park had discovered a crucial piece of evidence related to the assault on the Romaines. When they contacted her, the woman told police that she had seen a man and a boy run down a hill, only to stop briefly by a puddle of water. When she investigated, she discovered a man's shirt and tie lying there on the ground. Following her to the site, the police quickly bagged the evidence, which appeared to have bloodstains, for further testing, and then made a cast of a clear footprint discovered in the mud next to the puddle. The police were able to quickly trace the pair's escape route through the park, because it was littered with the bloody knife used to kill Fasching, more stolen goods, and a .32-caliber revolver that was identified as the man's gun.

In the meantime, the police thoroughly searched the Romaine home for additional evidence. They discovered some partial fingerprints, several rolls of adhesive tape, and the imprint of a bloody footprint. After canvassing the area, they spoke to a number of people who remembered the two strangers. Authorities later interviewed a bus driver who identified the man and boy as his passengers that day and acknowledged he had transported the pair to New York City. Although the police were not able to trace ownership of the knife or gun, the shirt proved to be a different story.

Not only did it turn out to have been made in Philadelphia, but a pale laundry mark ultimately revealed the letters "KAL."

The FBI was not able to identify the strangers' fingerprints that were taken from the Romaine house, but the Leonia murder was the impetus for authorities to begin a tri-state review of similar crimes in the Delaware Valley area. Sure enough, when Larry McClure, assistant prosecutor for Bergen County, issued a description of the pair, he received accounts of the same type of home invasions in other New Jersey towns, as well as in Maryland and Pennsylvania. Reports from the victims all agreed that the man who had forced his way into their homes exuded a strange, distinctive odor and was always accompanied by a young blond boy.

A false lead interrupted the police investigation less than a week after the Fasching murder. A Margate woman called police to say that a strange-smelling man with a knife, accompanied by a fair-haired boy, had forced their way into her home. Authorities were discouraged to find that she had made up the story. But they soon were encouraged by the fact that the discarded shirt with the "KAL" laundry mark had been cleaned and revealed a whole name: Kalinger. Although police could not find anyone with a criminal record by that name in their files, Detective Robert Roseman, who had been involved in the investigation from the start, took the shirt to Philadelphia and discovered it was sold only by the Berg Brothers store on North Front Street. But none of the store clerks recalled selling such a shirt to a dark-haired man who emitted a strange smell.

While he was in Philadelphia, Roseman checked the telephone book to see if he could find a listing for a Kalinger. No luck. But when he checked with the police department, he discovered that they had a record for a Kallinger. Armed with the right spelling, Roseman had better luck now. He visited different dry cleaners, and eventually the owner of Bright Sun on North Front Street was able to identify the shirt as belonging to Joseph Kallinger, who lived in the Kensington district. The smell apparently resulted from a chemical that the shoemaker used in his business.

Roseman soon learned that the cobbler was familiar to police, but little did he expect the tale of arson, child abuse, and the possibility of murder that they chronicled for him. When the detective shared his suspicions with the Philadelphia authorities, they soon organized a stakeout of the Kallinger home. In the meantime, a number of victims were able to identify Kallinger from a photograph as the man who had assaulted them. Although it was more difficult to positively identify his young companion, the police went ahead and arrested both Kallinger and Michael at home on January 17, 1976, a little more than one year since the day Maria Fasching was murdered. Kallinger was first charged with assault and robbery, but the Leonia police soon added murder to his growing list of crimes. While his father was held in Philadelphia to await trial, Michael was sent to a nearby juvenile facility until he turned twenty-one.

The police discovered some of the jewelry and valuables stolen during the pair's seven-week crime spree hidden in both Kallinger's home and his mother's next door. As they continued to gather evidence, authorities were positive the shoemaker was the right man. Although Kallinger refused at first to talk and his real motive remained a mystery, the police believed that the key factor behind his actions had simply been greed. They attempted to obtain testimony from Michael, but he remained as closemouthed as his father. The boy was never charged for his role in any of the crimes the pair allegedly committed and was not required to testify against his father. Michael, who later legally changed his name, eventually moved in with a foster family to try to forget his past. In the meantime, Elizabeth Kallinger told the press that the police were determined to frame her husband because he had successfully sued them for harassment. Kallinger's court-appointed attorney declared that the evidence against his client had been planted.

Kallinger remained silent for a while but apparently realized that he needed to establish some defense against the various charges he faced. Although he supposedly had a slightly below-average IQ, he was smart enough to tell authorities that his problems were caused by the devil, who had been chasing him for more than 1,000 years. He later said that God had directed him to make and distribute shoes for people whose brains weren't working properly because of poorly made footwear. Despite his best efforts to prove otherwise, the results of his neurological tests were all normal. After a two-hour examination by Dr. John Hume, Kallinger was diagnosed with anti-social personality disorder, not a real mental illness. Hume asserted that the shoemaker was faking insanity in an effort to avoid going to trial. In both New Jersey and Pennsylvania, a defendant has to have the mental capacity to tell the difference between right and wrong. If he can't, then he can qualify for an insanity defense.

In September 1976, Kallinger was tried in Pennsylvania on a variety of charges, including four counts of robbery, four counts of false imprisonment, and one count of burglary. He was convicted by the jury after less than an hour's deliberation and sentenced to thirty years in prison. With the first trial out of the way, authorities began extradition proceedings to have Kallinger stand trial in New Jersey for the murder of Maria Fasching. Apparently realizing that he was about to be held accountable for still more crimes, Kallinger waged a campaign that he believed would finally convince authorities that he was indeed insane. He vandalized his jail cell, threw excrement at the guards, and placed cups of water and urine under his bed. Despite his efforts, the doctors concluded Kallinger was faking. But Kallinger's new defense attorney, Paul Giblin, was prepared to present his own specialists for the defense. He asked Dr. Irwin Perrs from Rutgers University Medical School to interview Kallinger, and after a two-day examination, Perrs decided that the shoemaker was schiz-ophrenic and did not fully understand the nature of his crimes. As a result, he felt Kallinger should be eligible for an insanity defense.

Despite his apparently psychotic behavior, Kallinger again proved he was smart enough to know his defense might hinge on more than just adequate legal counsel. He wrote to Flora Rheta Schreiber, author of the best-selling book *Sybil,* about a woman who believed her body housed sixteen different personalities. Although some psychologists later cast doubt on her findings, Schreiber's book was an immediate best-seller that triggered new interest in mental disorders—so much so that the number of cases of multiple personality disorder, which had been very small up until that time, multiplied by about 1,000 percent. Schreiber, who had no professional training as a therapist, readily agreed to meet with the accused murderer and hear what he had to say. She was thrilled at the prospect of writing another book about such a unique psychosis, especially from a subject like Kallinger.

A professor of English and speech at City University of New York's John Jay College of Criminal Justice, Schreiber felt that her long-standing interest in abnormal psychology, plus the experience of writing her first book, was more than sufficient preparation for telling Kallinger's story. They met for the first time in 1976, while he was awaiting trial for Maria Fasching's murder. Although they initially mistrusted each other, Kallinger and Schreiber soon developed a relationship that went beyond the professional—ultimately coloring her account of his life. Just as she had in *Sybil,* Schreiber apparently relied as much on secondhand sources and her own opinion as she did on facts.

Schreiber believed Kallinger's account that his adoptive parents were cruel and unloving. He told her that they had once taken him for a hernia operation and said that the doctor had operated on his penis so it would never get hard. To Schreiber, this signified that his parents had symbolically "castrated" Kallinger, preventing him from ever being able to enjoy a normal boyhood. This treatment allegedly was what drove him to sexually assault a number of victims during his home invasions. In her book, Schreiber noted that Kallinger said his parents' abuse was also responsible for making him want to kill with a knife—it became his penis substitute, since he apparently was obsessed with the male organ.

Kallinger claimed that the voices in his head ordered him to kill 3 billion people but said it was Michael's fault that they mutilated and murdered ten-year-old Jose Collazo in July 1974. Kallinger told

Schreiber that they took the boy to an abandoned factory site, where they cut off his penis, then killed him by shoving a pair of shears into his rectum. Kallinger said he kept the dismembered penis. But it is more than possible that the shoemaker was just elaborating on a newspaper account of the child's murder, which described a slight laceration in the groin. He had not sustained injuries such as those Kallinger had described, but Schreiber apparently took his words at face value. In all likelihood, Kallinger's story was nothing more than another instance of his twisted imagination at work—still trying to convince someone that he was insane. Ironically, Kallinger might never have been charged with murdering his son, Joe Jr., and Jose Collazo if he hadn't confessed to committing both crimes to Schreiber.

Kallinger told Schreiber that he began to be haunted by "Charlie" the ghost, which he visualized as a severed head, the day he was contacted by the police about Joe Jr.'s death. Schreiber also conveniently ignored the fact that a large insurance settlement probably motivated Kallinger to commit such a crime. During one interview, Kallinger said that an angry Charlie commanded him to stab Maria Fasching after she refused to perform oral sex on Frank Welby. Kallinger saw the young nurse's death as a sign that his mission to annihilate the human race had begun. Schreiber chose to believe that the shoemaker was the victim of hallucinations, even though his memory was very clear for a man who was supposedly insane.

On September 13, 1976, Joseph Kallinger went on trial in Hackensack for the murder of Maria Fasching and other charges related to his invasion of the Romaine home, including assault, taking hostages, and the theft of property. Kallinger tried to prove he was insane by shouting and stamping his feet during the trial, but the jury was not impressed by his performance. In addition to their medical experts, the prosecution also had an assortment of physical evidence to present before the court: There were the shirt and tie that Kallinger had discarded in the park, together with a photograph of him wearing those same articles of clothing. There were Michael's fingerprints, lifted from a broken piggy bank at the

Romaine home. And most damning was the fact that all of Kallinger's victims who had been held hostage at the Romaines' that day readily identified the defendant as their assailant. On October 13, the jury found Kallinger guilty on all counts after just two hours of deliberation. The next day, he was again sentenced to life in prison, with the possibility of parole.

Kallinger was then transferred to Camden to face trial for the two home invasions he had committed within that county. But he continued to wage his campaign to try to prove he was a victim, not a criminal. In 1977, he was sent to the Psychiatric Hospital in Trenton for three weeks after he set fire to his cell. While undergoing more tests, he tried to suffocate himself with a piece of plastic. But all was to no avail—once again, his actions failed to convince neither the police nor the courts that he was insane. To safeguard the public, authorities imposed a life sentence without the possibility of parole on the shoemaker. But before he could begin serving his New Jersey sentences, Kallinger was returned to Pennsylvania to begin his first thirty-year term at the Huntington State Correctional Institution.

Unfortunately, Kallinger's story as related by Schreiber has all too often become accepted as fact, leading some to believe that he was as much a victim of violence as those he terrorized. Although convicted of at least one murder, and possibly guilty of more, whether he was actually a serial killer—or even psychotic—is anyone's guess. The professionals could not agree then, and they still cannot satisfactorily establish a motive for Kallinger's behavior.

Initially isolated, the shoemaker was eventually deemed stable enough to join the general prison population. But a few months later, he stabbed and strangled another prisoner and went on a hunger strike. It seems that after years of trying, he finally managed to convince prison authorities that he was in fact insane. He was moved in 1978 to Farview State Hospital, a Pennsylvania maximum-security mental hospital for the criminally insane. Officially diagnosed as paranoid schizophrenic, Kallinger spent his days sleeping, writing poetry, or repairing shoes. According to his therapist, Dr. Ralph E. Davis, the shoemaker felt a lot of remorse for his criminal actions. In 1996 at age fifty-nine, Joseph Kallinger died at the hospital from a seizure, taking the truth with him.

* * *

In the years that followed, other heinous crimes occurred throughout the state of New Jersey. One that drew widespread public attention was the shooting death of State Trooper Philip Lamonaco, age thirty-two, who was killed on December 21, 1981, by Thomas Manning and Richard Williams, two survivalists who were wanted on a variety of criminal charges. The two men were later captured. Manning was convicted, but a hung jury meant that Williams had to be retried before he, too, was convicted. Both men received life sentences.

Another, according to Gerald Tomlinson in *Murder in New Jersey,* was a mystery that remains unresolved even today. Andrew Puskas of Middlesex Borough telephoned the police on February 25, 1982, to inform them that someone had delivered a pipe bomb to his house. Although he had time to save his children, both Puskas and his wife, Patricia, died in the explosion that ripped through their ranch-style home. In his book, Tomlinson stated: "A neighbor had seen a stranger in a white station wagon, with a large package visible in the back, driving slowly through the neighborhood at about 8:05 A.M. The driver, a man, pulled into either the Puskas driveway or a driveway next door." Unfortunately, the clue did not lead authorities to the criminal, and to date, no one knows who murdered Puskas and his wife or why the suburban family was targeted.

A few years later, another crime destroyed the Marshalls, a Garden State family who, on the surface at least, appeared to have it all. What horrified most people, however, was the fact that the cause of their destruction did not come from a mysterious stranger, but from within. Unlike John List, however, the father of this family did not choose to pick up a gun and commit the crime himself.

CHAPTER 5
Contract Killers

✳ ✳ ✳

Maria Marshall took her marriage vows seriously and tried to be a good wife and loving mother. She never realized that her husband saw "till death do us part" as a loophole in their marriage contract that he could exercise in order to pursue a new life with another woman.

On March 5, 1986, prominent Toms River businessman Robert Marshall was convicted of the murder of his wife, Maria, even though he didn't actually pull the trigger of the gun used to shoot her twice in the back. It seems that Marshall, who received the death penalty for his part in the murder, instead hired two contract killers to commit the heinous crime for him. In the aftermath, many New Jersey residents wondered how he could destroy his own family in such a cold-blooded fashion. But it was fairly simple. What should have been a modern-day fairy tale turned into a daytime soap opera when lust and greed were interjected into the story. And two decades after that fatal night, there is still no happy ending on the horizon.

The tragedy became a cautionary tale for others who, at that time, considered conspicuous consumption to be a major life goal.

According to Joe McGinnis, who chronicled Marshall's crime in *Blind Faith,* this included most of the nouveau riche of Toms River. Like many Americans, they quickly succumbed to the lure of the "greed is good" philosophy that ran rampant in the 1980s. And the Marshalls apparently were no exception.

How could something that seemed to start out so right end so badly?

When Robert Marshall began to court Maria Puszynski in the early 1960s, he appeared to be a smart, ambitious man who could make all her dreams come true. She fell in love with his bright, outgoing personality and was delighted when he finally managed to convince her conservative parents that he would make a good husband. Although the Puszynskis had their doubts, they ultimately conceded, and on December 28, 1963, the young couple was married at St. Adalbert's Church in Philadelphia.

Marshall had barely scraped through his classes to graduate from Villanova University, but he was determined to make his mark on the world. He joined the Navy after college and discovered Toms River while stationed at the Naval Air Station in nearby Lakehurst. The upper-income, suburban community on the New Jersey coast had been created out of barren sand dunes and swamp in the 1950s. Home building and businesses raced to eat up the land, and Marshall liked the idea of setting down roots in a booming town that encouraged and supported ambitious growth and development. Property was readily available at the time, and in 1973, the Marshalls moved into a new home with an in-ground forty-foot pool built especially for them on a quarter-acre lot in the prestigious Brookside section of town.

The Marshalls and their three sons soon became fixtures at the Toms River Country Club, socializing with other young families who also enjoyed the finer things in life. For a while it seemed as though the attractive pair had just about everything their hearts could desire—a family, money, a beautiful home, and the respect and admiration of their neighbors. Being established in such a close-knit community was very important to Marshall, who, as the oldest of five children, had been dragged from town to town by his restless, alcoholic father. The family had always seemed to be just one step ahead of the bill collectors. A part of him probably also recognized that Maria, the beloved only child of a doctor and his wife, had enjoyed a more privileged upbringing, so he wanted to prove he could be a success.

Marshall quickly became one of Provident Mutual Insurance Company's top salesmen, earning a $12,000 bonus for selling $2 million worth of insurance policies during his first year with the Philadelphia-based firm. To flaunt their success, the couple bought an expensive car and an eighteen-foot ski boat christened the *Double Down*. But no matter how much they spent, Rob, the consummate businessman, always seemed to be involved in yet another deal. Whether it was to "keep up with the Joneses" or just Rob's ambition, the Marshalls seemed determined to provide themselves and their boys with the best that money could buy. Actively involved in civic affairs, the Marshalls always participated in fund-raisers thrown by the United Way or the country club. They attended many of their sons' extracurricular activities, leading the cheers for the teams.

When they weren't at the Toms River Country Club, the couple would speed south on the Garden State Parkway to Atlantic City. The Queen of Resorts had just undergone a facelift, thanks to the advent of casino gambling, and Marshall enjoyed nothing more than spending hundreds, sometimes thousands, at the blackjack tables. According to McGinnis, he also derived pleasure from showing off his beautiful wife: "He seemed even more proud of her than of his Cadillac, and she, it must be said, appeared quite flattered to be treated as an ornament." But beneath the surface, the once-happy marriage seemed to have lost its allure for Marshall. He was bored. Although they still socialized, Maria seemed more caught up in the lives of their children and running the household than she was in him. Up early every day to cook breakfast and tend to the needs of her family, she would be curled up on the couch most nights, just about the time that he was ready to go out and enjoy some nightlife.

But Marshall continued to go through the motions, until the Fourth of July weekend in 1983, when he and Maria were attending a friend's barbecue. That was when his attention was captured by Sarann Kraushaar, a part-time aerobics instructor and vice principal at a local high school. Although she was married at the time to a local automobile dealer, the vivacious brunette quickly responded to Marshall's attention, and before long, the two began a torrid affair. The couple exchanged tape-recorded love notes, and after a year of clandestine meetings, they decided to leave their spouses and set up housekeeping together.

Although Kraushaar later told authorities that she didn't think much of the comment at the time, she said that in December 1983, Marshall said he wished Maria was not around to stand in their way. Marshall claimed that Kraushaar, in turn, provided him with the name of another local resident who was reputed to have ties to organized crime in Ocean County—in other words, someone who could possibly grant his wish. As it turned out, Marshall didn't use Kraushaar's alleged connection. But all the same, the idea—mentioned so casually in conversation—apparently never left his mind.

At about this time, it seems that Maria had discovered evidence of her husband's affair. Worse yet, she also became aware that the family was sliding ever deeper into debt because of Marshall's reckless spending. In addition to finding out about unpaid bills and a number of personal loans, she was shocked to learn that her husband had forged her name on a $100,000 home equity loan application. Authorities later discovered that before Maria died, Marshall had spent more than twice his annual salary of $100,000 a year, his gambling debts were mounting, and he owed $80,000 on a mortgage held on an office. She apparently shared her concerns with Gene Leahy, a family friend and an attorney. Unknown to her husband, she also hired a private investigator to look further into Marshall's activities. Although Maria reportedly planned to confront her husband about his recent behavior, according to McGinnis, it was only to try to save her marriage. But after the incident of the missing money, she never got the chance. Divorce, once a viable option for Marshall, receded as another plan took shape—one that would resolve all of his problems.

In early 1984, after a bad night at the tables in Atlantic City, Marshall asked Maria to give him $3,500, which amounted to her share of their gambling funds. He wanted to use the money to cover that night's debt at the casino. Maria told him the money had already been spent, and at the time, Marshall thought no further about it. But shortly afterward, Kraushaar told him a mutual friend had alerted her that Maria had her suspicions about his constant business trips, which were a smokescreen for their affair. Marshall, worried that his wife would pay a private detective to follow him, knew he was in danger of losing everything—his home, his family, and his status in the community. He decided to seek outside help.

On May 24 of that same year, Marshall met Robert Cumber, a hardware store clerk from Bossier City, Louisiana, at a neighbor's party. Although there were an endless number of reputable agencies to choose from in the Delaware Valley area, Marshall claimed that he later contacted Cumber about hiring a private investigator from Louisiana to trail Maria. He was probably trying to find out just what his wife knew about his activities, but Marshall later told authorities that he had just been seeking help to track the missing $3,500, for which Maria couldn't account. Cumber, in turn, put Marshall in touch with another Louisiana native, Billy Wayne McKinnon, who offered to help—even though McKinnon wasn't really serious at the time.

To McKinnon, the rich New Jerseyan was ripe for the plucking, so he was only to happy to travel to an Atlantic City casino on June 18 to meet with Marshall. During the meeting, Marshall allegedly paid McKinnon a $7,000 retainer to follow Maria and see what she was up to. But before the night ended, they also agreed that Cumber and McKinnon would split $65,000 if they successfully murdered Marshall's wife as soon as possible. McKinnon returned to Louisiana $7,000 richer and happy to ignore Marshall's detailed information about Maria's daily schedule. After all, it wasn't as though his "client" could go to the police and report him for taking the money.

But the retainer apparently wasn't enough for the petty criminal. He returned to New Jersey the following month in an effort to acquire a little more of Marshall's money. Marshall, desperate to prove his sincerity, gave McKinnon an additional $7,000, and they decided that the murder would take place in the parking lot of an Atlantic City diner. Not surprisingly, McKinnon once again failed to appear, although he later claimed that he waited in the parking lot for almost an hour. When the Marshalls allegedly didn't show, he drove back to his home state. That August, McKinnon said, he was contacted by Larry Thompson, an acquaintance with a criminal past, who told him he had been hired to kill McKinnon for not following through on another shady deal. McKinnon then proceeded to enlist the man's help in milking more money from Marshall, although Thompson's role in the New Jersey murder was later disputed.

Did Marshall finally realize that he had selected the wrong partner for his plan? Apparently not, because on September 6, he once again met with McKinnon at a Garden State Parkway rest stop. From there the two men rode down the highway to try to find just the right spot to commit murder. They finally agreed that the Oyster Creek Picnic Area was suitably dark and desolate. Ironically, it was this location, which may have seemed right at the time, that raised an immediate red flag for the police. After all, if the Marshalls really did have a bad tire, as Marshall later claimed, why would he pull the car so far off the highway where help would have been readily available?

That fateful evening, as they had done so many times before, the couple sped down the Garden State Parkway in their big yellow Cadillac Eldorado to Atlantic City to enjoy an evening on the town.

After an elaborate dinner and several hours of gambling at Harrah's Casino, they headed toward home shortly after midnight on September 7. But Maria would never see her three beloved sons or her elegant suburban house again. According to McKinnon, he and Thompson followed Marshall's car after he saw it cross the tollgates near the Oyster Creek Picnic Area. As they approached the heavily wooded site, he let Thompson out, then waited a few minutes before pulling in behind the Cadillac. McKinnon later told authorities that by the time he arrived, he could see Marshall lying near the rear of the Cadillac. Just then, Thompson came crashing through the underbrush and threw a few things into McKinnon's car, before returning to slash a tire on Marshall's vehicle. He said the two took off south down the parkway, dumping a .45-caliber handgun and Maria's purse out the window as they fled the scene of the crime.

When the police arrived, they discovered Marshall nursing a blow to his head that later required five stitches. But Maria had not been so fortunate. Her body was slumped across the front seat of the Cadillac, shot twice in the back. Although Marshall claimed that her death probably was the result of a mugging gone fatally wrong, authorities quickly became suspicious. In his book, McGinnis noted that a number of friends and neighbors doubted the story almost immediately, because Marshall's account of the murder kept changing every time he related it. Why, they wondered, would he pull into such an isolated area, allegedly to change a tire, when everyone knew he preferred to pay for such services? Although they were at first sympathetic, even his two older sons grew concerned, especially after Marshall admitted that he had been having an affair.

Suspicion grew after the police realized that Marshall wasn't able to give them a consistent report about what had happened that night. And when investigators from the Ocean County Prosecutor's Office uncovered his relationship with Kraushaar, they learned that Marshall had taken a long-distance call from Louisiana one night at her apartment. Kraushaar told authorities that she became suspicious when he claimed it was in reference to a gambling debt. Familiar with Marshall's crumbling finances, she became concerned that something was drastically wrong. For her, their burning passion was quickly doused by the reality that he might have been involved in Maria's murder. With the exception of her court appearances, Kraushaar never saw her former lover again.

The once top insurance salesman probably realized by then that the authorities were piecing together the puzzle to get a clear picture of Maria's death. With the law closing in and his relationship over, Marshall checked into a motel room in Lakewood and recorded a suicide tape. But the suicide—probably initiated as a dramatic gesture to show his unstable state of mind—never happened. Rescue workers arrived just in time to get him to a local hospital, where he rapidly recuperated. As it turned out, he would need all his strength in the weeks ahead.

Marshall was dismayed by the fact that his contacts in Louisiana quickly came to light. On September 22, Cumber was arrested and charged as an accomplice in a conspiracy to commit murder. A few weeks later, McKinnon and James Davis of Shreveport were arrested and also charged with conspiracy to commit murder. The three men were indicted on October 17 on the charge, with McKinnon additionally charged with committing the actual murder. Davis was indicted as an accomplice. By mid-December, McKinnon agreed to cooperate with authorities and, in return for his plea bargain, received five years in the prison of his choice. McKinnon later told police that Larry Thompson was the person who actually shot Maria.

Robert Marshall, once a devoted family man and well-known civic leader, was arrested on December 19, 1984, and charged with solicitation of murder and as an accomplice to the crime. According to McGinnis: "It wasn't until later—until too late—that people looked back and realized that maybe she'd become a slave to his vision of her and to the image she was trying to project. That her obsession with appearances might have cost her her life." Maria apparently became a status symbol to her husband, rather than a person, which was an unforgivable mistake and the main reason why the rest of the town turned against Marshall after her death. "In Toms River," McGinnis noted, "you're supposed to take better care of your possessions." While Marshall was held in lieu of $2 million bail, Thompson was arrested and charged with Maria's murder.

The media frenzy that surrounded the case forced Superior Court Judge William H. Huber to grant the defense a change of venue on April 25, 1985. As a result, the trial was moved to the Atlantic County Court House in Mays Landing, Atlantic County's small county seat. On July 16, the charge of acting as an accomplice was dismissed against Cumber by Atlantic County Superior Court Judge Manuel H. Greenberg, although he still had to answer to the charge of conspiracy.

When the case came to court on January 20, 1986, Marshall and Thompson were tried as co-defendants before a jury of eleven men and five women. Marshall's lawyer was Glenn A. Zeitz of Philadelphia, and Thompson's attorney was Francis J. Hartman of Mount Holly. Assistant Ocean County Prosecutor Kevin W. Kelly bluntly advised the jury that Marshall had his wife killed to collect roughly $1.5 million in insurance policy premiums. His motive? The money would have been more than sufficient to erase about $300,000 in personal debt and provide him with a comfortable nest egg for the future Mrs. Marshall.

The defense attorneys charged that the state's case was based on false statements made by McKinnon. But McKinnon was not the only witness for the prosecution. During the trial, several insurance agents testified that Marshall had asked them to write policies on Maria's life within eight months prior to her death. Perhaps the most damning testimony was offered by Marshall himself, when he testified on February 23. Although he denied any involvement in his wife's shooting, he showed a cold, calculating face to the jury when he admitted that not only had he had an affair while his wife was

THE BIG HOUSE

The New Jersey State Prison that is located in Trenton today is the latest in a long line of penitentiaries that have stood off Route 129 since the late eighteenth century. The first prison was constructed in 1799 on six-and-a-half acres in the area of Trenton once known as Lamberton. The prison was modeled after the Walnut Street Jail in Philadelphia, which was designed according to the Quaker philosophy that solitary confinement allowed prisoners the opportunity to reflect on and repent their crimes. Men, women, and sometimes children, including people who were mentally ill or physically disabled, all were housed within the prison walls. According to former prison guard Harry Camisa in *Inside Out: Fifty Years Behind the Walls of New Jersey's Trenton State Prison,* "After 30 years of mixing all types of prisoners in one building, politicians and prison administrations concluded the congregate system was unworkable." As a result, construction of a new, more updated prison was started in 1834 and finished four years later.

The second penitentiary was designed by English architect John Haviland, who was well known for designing prisons. The Trenton facility was the second prison built in the United States that was modeled on the Pennsyl-

alive, but he also had several romantic encounters immediately after her death.

The following day, Thompson told the court that he had been in Louisiana at the time of the slaying and produced a number of witnesses to support his story. He was later acquitted of the charges against him.

When the assistant prosecutor gave his summation the following week, it was obvious that he was completely affronted by Marshall's behavior. Kelly not only declared the defendant a coward, but also noted that there was "a place in hell" for him. That same day, the jury convicted Marshall of all charges against him and, after only ninety additional minutes of deliberation, sentenced him to death.

vania system of solitary confinement. According to www.memory.loc.gov: "It was the first building in the United States to exhibit characteristics of Egyptian revival architectures, possible the first American building to directly influence the architecture of Europe. Technologically, it was perhaps the first American building to utilize a system of hot water heating."

The seventeen-acre facility grew along with the prison population, which increased to almost 200 inmates by 1845. By 1869, a separate wing for women was added, along with a large workshop where inmates were expected to learn a trade. By that time, the solitary confinement philosophy had been discarded in favor of one that promoted work rather than isolation. A separate death row and execution chamber were added to the site after state legislators decided in 1907 that all executions would take place at the state prison instead of individual county jails.

In 1977, the state decided to tear down the second prison and build a new facility to house the ever-growing inmate population. Some of the unique design elements were documented before they were destroyed, and others were incorporated into the new prison. To see pictures and learn more about the history of the prison, visit the Library of Congress's Historic American Buildings Survey site at www.loc.gov.

In New Jersey, the degree of cruelty involved in the death and contracting for murder are two of eleven aggravating factors that allow prosecutors to seek the death penalty if a defendant is found guilty. Those circumstances are balanced against such mitigating concerns as whether the accused suffers from a mental illness or has a previous criminal record. Although Marshall had demonstrated apparent unstable behavior with his aborted suicide attempt and until that time had no criminal history, the jury unanimously decided that his crimes merited the ultimate punishment.

In June, Cumber was found guilty of being an accomplice to murder and was sentenced to life with the possibility of parole after thirty years. The following month, McKinnon pleaded guilty to conspiracy to kill Maria. In exchange for testifying for the prosecution, he received a five-year sentence with credit for time served. As a result, he was paroled from jail on October 7 of that same year.

Marshall, who might have been the first man to be executed by lethal injection in New Jersey since the death penalty was revived in 1982, was transferred to death row at the New Jersey State Prison in Trenton following his conviction. For more than twenty years, he insisted that he had not hired contract killers from Louisiana to execute his wife so that he could collect enough insurance money to pay off his debts. As he repeatedly appealed his sentence, Marshall decided that it was time to set the record—which had been adversely influenced by *Blind Faith*—straight, so he wrote his own book, titled *Tunnel Vision,* about his arrest and subsequent trial.

Although there may have been times when he gave up hope after so many years, in the end, his perseverance was rewarded. In 2004, just when Marshall had almost completely exhausted the appeal process and was dangerously close to being scheduled for execution, Judge Joseph E. Irenas of the U.S. District Court decreed that he was entitled to another trial for the death penalty phase of his case. Irenas decreed that Marshall had not been competently represented by counsel during the original sentencing process. In a sixty-page ruling handed down on April 4, the judge ordered a reprieve because he determined that the defendant's attorney had failed to act in the best interests of his client. In the judge's opinion, Marshall had been unfairly forced to face a jury less than two hours after collapsing outside the courtroom. An hour after the conclusion of the death penalty phase of his trial, that jury voted that Marshall deserved to die for his crimes.

Irenas's ruling, which stunned most New Jersey residents, was upheld the following year by the U.S. Third Circuit Court of Appeals. Although some questioned whether Marshall was just benefiting from a change in public opinion regarding the death penalty, after more than two decades, he was no longer in danger of dying by lethal injection. After receiving the court's ruling, Ocean County Prosecutor Thomas Kelaher decided it would not be possible to successfully prosecute Marshall again after so much time had passed. He advised the court that his office would no longer seek the death penalty but recommended a life sentence without the possibility of parole.

In 2006, acting New Jersey governor Richard Codey signed a moratorium on the death penalty and pardoned Cumber for his part in the Marshall crime. That August, Marshall was sentenced to life in prison with the possibility of parole after thirty years. Because the sixty-five-year-old inmate had by that time already served twenty-two years behind bars, he could be a free man by 2014.

* * *

While Robert Marshall campaigned to avoid the death penalty, a self-described "ninja killer" conducted a campaign of terror between 1988 and 1991 in Montville, a small suburban community in northern New Jersey just across the river from New York. During his crime spree, thirty-five-year-old Joseph M. Harris of Paterson, an unemployed postal worker, committed murder, rape, robbery, and assault against people he felt had wronged him in business deals. According to Gerald Tomlinson in *Murder in New Jersey,* Harris later told authorities that he believed a ninja spirit, which helped him survive a difficult childhood, inhabited his body. Convicted on murder charges by a Morris County jury, Harris was given the death penalty. He is currently an inmate on death row at the New Jersey State Prison in Trenton.

CHAPTER 6
Mob Rule

✳ ✳ ✳

You don't have to be a fan of the television show to recognize the name of Tony Soprano, the angst-ridden North Jersey Mafioso who rules his fictional crime family with an iron fist. Tony might be among the first of his kind to spend time in a therapist's office, but his inner hoodlum is readily released whenever he has to order someone killed or even do the job himself.

When David Chase's television series first aired on HBO in 1999, it stunned many people with its intimate, seemingly accurate presentation of modern-day mob life. As it turned out, the North Jersey native who authored the show, born David DeCaesare, didn't have to go far for his inspiration. Chase grew up in Soprano territory and mined his memories to create a riveting, Emmy award-winning drama.

But who were the people behind the characters? Did they, in fact, live and behave like Tony Soprano and his crew?

To better understand the real modern-day criminal syndicate that inspired the creation of *The Sopranos,* it is necessary to turn the clock back to the late nineteenth century, when New Jersey attracted the second-largest wave of Italian immigrants after New York. While many stayed in the industrial cities of the northern part of the state, working in clothing factories and at the ports, others were attracted to the rolling acres of open farmland in the south, which were reminiscent of their homeland. Although the majority of them were honest and industrious, there were some who preferred a life of crime to one of hard work. These criminals soon organized into a confederation that became commonly known as the Mafia. And unfortunately, no matter where they settled, the Italian immigrants often found that their lives were still shadowed by men who were part of this group. The secret organization, which had existed in Italy since the 1800s, was firmly established in America by the early twentieth century. New York became the center of their power, but a shoot from the ever-expanding criminal syndicate was soon planted in the Garden State.

Historians have documented the fact that a small segment of every ethnic group has chosen a life of crime, dating to the earliest days of immigration. They usually organized on a small scale to protect neighborhood residents from other groups or what they perceived as corrupt authorities. In *Gangs of New York,* author Herbert Asbury recounted how different gangs, divided on ethnic and racial lines, waged bloody battles in the nineteenth century over sections of the city that they considered their turf. What made the Mafia different was the scope and style of its organization—one that seemed to reflect modern-day corporate structure. Not loners, as depicted in the old Clint Eastwood spaghetti westerns, these men were soldiers in a vast phantom network whose reach extended from the darkest alleys to the well-lit, carpeted halls of political power. As a result, the Mafia—also known over the years as Il Cosa Nostra, La Familia, the Black Hand, or the Mob—seems to not only have survived but thrived since the first Italians arrived in the New World.

New Jersey's first family of organized crime was the DeCavalcantes, whose operations were primarily concentrated in Essex, Union, Bergen, and Hudson Counties. While other mafioso conducted business throughout the Garden State, the DeCavalcantes were the first family to headquarter here. For many years, they were led by Simone Rizzo DeCavalcante, who was born on May 3, 1912, in Brooklyn but moved with his family at an early age to Trenton. He grew up to become known as "Sam the Plumber," a dapper, gracious, old-school mob leader, according to those who knew him, who was as much concerned about proper manners among the young as he was about extorting money from local businesses. DeCavalcante, who was said to have been one of the models for Mario Puzo's character Don Vito Corleone in his classic novel *The Godfather,* owned about six different companies in North Jersey. But his real fortune was amassed through a criminal empire ruled out of his plumbing supply store in Kenilworth. During his reign, the DeCavalcantes were not considered as bloodthirsty as some families in other states, but that didn't mean their boss wasn't above ordering or committing violence when he felt it was necessary. Although the bloody street wars waged during Prohibition might have been over, sometimes it was necessary to show both his enemies and his allies who was in charge.

Inducted into the Mafia as a young man, DeCavalcante assumed command of the New Jersey Mafia in 1954 after the death of his uncle, mob leader Nicholas Delmore of Long Branch. At that time, the mob family, which traced its roots to Sicily, had been established for about twenty years. Delmore, who rose to power in the 1930s, was a brewery owner and local political boss who had managed to avoid prosecution on conspiracy and murder charges. Not long after DeCavalcante's ascension, the family was christened with his name by the Kefauver Committee, which had been established by the federal government to investigate organized crime. The committee stated that the DeCavalcantes were responsible for illegal gambling, union racketeering, loan-sharking, and other nefarious activities in the state. The family's criminal enterprises netted them millions of dollars in profit that the government was unable to touch. The committee, which met for more than a year, questioned more than 800 witnesses throughout the country. According to www.history.acusd.edu, "The hearings popularized the legend of a highly-organized crime family called the 'mafia' imported from Sicily." But there was nothing mythical about this particular legend—at least, not in New Jersey. The state had long been a haven for illegal activity of all sorts. Before long, federal authorities declared that the Mafia was spreading its tentacles farther than it ever had before, which included the Garden State. It seemed that in DeCavalcante's case, they weren't far wrong.

Under his leadership, family membership doubled to about sixty "soldiers," as lower-ranking mob members were commonly known. DeCavalcante also expanded the mob's influence over illegal gambling and labor union activity throughout the state. It was said that the success of any construction project in New Jersey hinged on his good will—if he was crossed, a job site could suddenly be shut down by labor troubles or a lack of supplies. Although not as high profile as some of his counterparts in New York and Philadelphia, the Princeton Township resident apparently enjoyed his chosen lifestyle. He was reputed to be a low-key person, often preferring not to travel with an entourage. Respected as something of a statesman, DeCavalcante sometimes mediated disputes between other branches of the Mafia.

In the 1960s, it was believed that more than twenty Mafia families were operating in America. Their activities were reportedly controlled by the heads of the Five Families of New York, known as the Mafia Commission, which included the Bonannos, Colombos, Gambinos, Genoveses, and Luccheses. In an effort to learn more about the Mafia's all-pervasive influence, government officials targeted DeCavalcante because he was known to have had contact with a number of different mob figures. In addition, he was considered a pioneer of sophisticated labor racketeering schemes. Acting upon the orders of Director J. Edgar Hoover, the FBI illegally wiretapped his business between 1961 and 1965 and accumulated the "Goodfella Tapes," which—in DeCavalcante's own words—revealed the names and other sometimes disturbing details about members of the

Mafia Commission. The tapes supported information that had been previous provided to the federal government by Joe Valachi, a low-level mob member who was one of the first to break the *omerta,* the Mafia code of silence. Federal authorities compiled about 2,300 typewritten pages of transcript, which included conversations between DeCavalcante and corrupt officials and discussions with his men about their influence over local businesses and union activity, as well as extortion, gambling, bribery, and, of course, murder.

In *Blood and Honor: Inside the Scarfo Mob—the Mafia's Most Violent Family,* author George Anastasia noted that the tapes included information on a "slot machine scam" set up by the Genovese family in North Jersey, which brought in millions over a four-year period. The tapes also linked local politicians like Thomas Dunn, who was the mayor of Elizabeth, and Joseph "Joe Bayonne" Zicarelli, "the mob boss of the Jersey waterfront," with the DeCavalcantes. During one recorded discussion with DeCavalcante, Zicarelli expressed his concern that his former friend, Senator Harrison Williams, had become noticeably distant after Zicarelli was arrested six years earlier. In another, DeCavalcante's associates Angelo "Gyp" DeCarlo and Anthony "Tony Boy" Boiardo chillingly detailed how they had committed a murder.

The tapes were released to the public in 1969, and shortly afterward, DeCavalcante, the man who had avoided jail all his life, was imprisoned on charges of extortion and conspiracy. According to www.ganglandnews.com, when he was released in 1976, the former head of the New Jersey mob retired to South Florida. He had intended to open a string of casinos there, but his plans were thwarted when Florida residents, obviously still harboring memories of the well-publicized Kefauver Committee hearings, voted against legalized gambling. DeCavalcante died in 1997 at age eighty-four and was buried at Greenwood Cemetery in Hamilton.

A number of mob figures were jailed in the 1970s, as federal officials engaged in a crackdown throughout the United States. But the Mafia's degeneration at that time was caused as much by internal forces as external ones. According to Greg B. Smith, author of *Made Men: The True Rise-and-Fall Story of a New Jersey Mob Family:*

> The Colombo family had been torn up in Brooklyn street wars, and its members were being prosecuted one by one. The Luchese family had gone underground after one of its middle managers decided to try and shoot the sister of an informant—violating mob rules. The Bonanno clan degenerated after being kicked out of the Commission—the mob's ruling body. The Genovese family lacked leadership. The most powerful family at that time, the Gambino family, was brought down by its boss, John Gotti, "the dapper Don." Although he managed to avoid prosecution for years, in 1992 he was convicted of murder and racketeering and everything else. His own words, captured by FBI bugs, had brought him down.

Even with all of its apparent success, the federal government did not forget to keep an electronic eye on the DeCavalcantes. And with good reason. The New Jersey mob was still raking in profits from all types of businesses, both legal and illegal, without providing Uncle Sam with his fair share. In his book, Anastasia revealed that surveillance disclosed that in one instance the "Bonnano and DeCavalcante crime family leaders were linked to a junket operation that generated an estimated $6 million in kickbacks and payoffs before it was uncovered by the state police."

Although the government believed that mass arrests would decimate the power structure of the Mafia, for every man that was imprisoned, another was standing by ready to take his place. In New Jersey, DeCavalcante named John Riggi as his successor, and Riggi assumed command of the family the same year the former mob boss retired. According to www.mafianj.com, "John Riggi had been business agent for Local 394 from 1965 to 1986 and then president of District Council 30 in 1986." After his "retirement," Riggi's union connections allegedly allowed the DeCavalcante family to "extort jobs, goods and services from the construction industry in New Jersey." A report from the New Jersey Commission of Investigation stated, "If a general contractor opts to pay a bribe to a corrupt union business agent, either in cash or in goods and services, he can do a job with non-union labor, saving 30-40% in salaries alone, as well as the cost of fringe benefits normally paid into union welfare and pension funds." When he wasn't involved with family business, Riggi could sometimes be found accompanying John Gotti, head of the Gambinos, around New York's Little Italy. More flamboyant than his predecessor, Riggi was determined to prove that his family deserved the Mafia Commission's respect. For various reasons, such as disputes over profits or territory, the New Jersey faction had not always found favor with New York's powerful bosses. Riggi seemed determined to improve that relationship. But just as it had in the past, electronic surveillance proved to be the undoing of another DeCavalcante boss.

At the conclusion of a three-year federal investigation based in large part on wiretapped phones and listening devices, Riggi was jailed in 1990 on a variety of charges that included racketeering, conspiracy, extortion, and the obstruction of justice. In a joint press release issued at that time by state and federal officials, Mary Joe White, the U.S. Attorney for the Southern District of New York, stated:

> The Decavalcante Organized Crime Family is one of the oldest and most entrenched La Cosa Nostra Families in the Nation. These charges represent the first time that the Decavalcante Family's top leadership has been charged with such broad racketeering activity, including numerous acts of violence. In our continuing effort to eradicate the corrupt influence of all of La Cosa Nostra throughout the metropolitan area, the effect of this prosecution will be to dismantle the leadership of the Decavalcante Family and significantly diminish the Family's power base in New York and New Jersey.

Riggi was given special dispensation in 2000 to leave prison to pay his last respects to his wife, Sarah, after she died of cancer. Accompanied by U.S. marshals, he was permitted a private viewing before being escorted back to the Metropolitan Correctional Center in Lower Manhattan. Although he had been imprisoned for a decade by that time, federal officials believed that Riggi still ran the DeCavalcante family businesses from his prison cell. The aging mob leader, who suffered from a heart condition, was later moved to the Federal Medical Center Devens outside Boston. Even though he was initially supposed to be released in 2002, he remained incarcerated when informants provided testimony that allowed the government to press additional charges against him. In 2003, Riggi pleaded guilty to conspiring to murder real estate developer Fred Weiss, who had been shot to death outside his Staten Island home on September 11, 1989. Weiss apparently had crossed the Gambino family, and they were afraid he would be persuaded to turn state's evidence against them at an upcoming hearing. The next anticipated release date of the former mob leader, age eighty-one as of this writing, is scheduled for 2012.

After he went to jail, Riggi selected John D'Amato as acting boss, but his choice did not sit well with some of the other DeCavalcante family members, who thought that their new leader didn't have the right skills to take charge. When they later learned that he was homosexual, D'Amato's reign was abruptly ended in a hail of bullets, according to several informants. His body was never found, however. He was replaced by Giacomo "Jake" Amari, who, like Riggi, was deeply involved in manipulating the labor unions. Amari, who ran AMI Construction in Elizabeth, was considered another old-school mafioso, leading the family until he died of stomach cancer in 1997. His death left a vacancy that other mobsters were determined to fill. One of them was Charles "Big Ears" Majuri, according to www.answers.com, a longtime member who felt that he had been disrespected by the family when he wasn't invited to participate in a panel that Riggi organized to lead the DeCavalcantes. Murderous plots were hatched on all sides, but Majuri avoided execution at the last moment when the hitmen sent after him decided they did not have the right opportunity to commit murder.

Besides warding off the government, over the years the DeCavalcantes sometimes found themselves confronted by members of other families who wanted a taste of their illegal earnings. Conflict also arose when the Mafia Commission discovered that in the past, Sam the Plumber had altered some aspects of the time-honored initiation ceremony. In order to maintain their status as mafiosi, many of the DeCavalcantes had to be inducted again under the watchful eye of the New York bosses. Additional difficulties occurred on occasion with the Scarfo family of Philadelphia, which reportedly controlled a highly profitable vending-machine company that had a monopoly on video machines in New Jersey.

Murder seemed to be considered a useful tool that was sometimes used on family members who violated Mafia rules. According to www.mafia.com:

> Vincent "Jimmy" Rotundo, once the second-in-command of the DeCavalcante family and an organizer for Local 1814 of the Longshoreman's Union, was killed in Brooklyn in January 1988. Law enforcement sources say one motive for Rotundo's murder may have been because he had introduced into the family an individual who has since become a federally protected government informant and testified against Riggi. Because of Rotundo's rank within the DeCavalcante/Riggi organization, this homicide was most likely sanctioned by both Riggi and Gambino family boss John Gotti.

Traditionally, a "made man," one who had been initiated into the Mafia, could not be killed without prior approval of the Commission. But as the Mafia's structure was fractured by more arrests and internal dissension, arguments were sometimes settled with murder, and not always with the blessing of the Commission, as had been required in times past.

As the older generations either went to jail or died, new leadership continued to emerge from within the ranks. One such man was Vincent "Vinny Ocean" Palermo, who in 1965 had married DeCavalcante's niece. Palermo, who reportedly acquired his nickname because he had worked in a fish market as a youth, was initiated at age twenty into the ranks as a soldier. DeCavalcante liked Palermo and began inviting him to the local social club where he and other family members spent time. Modeling his behavior after his uncle's, he quietly established himself as a man to be reckoned with. Palermo soon gained control of a number of legal businesses, including gentlemen's clubs in New York, and illegal activities, such as loan-sharking and gambling in North Jersey. According to www.ganglandnews.com, Palermo gained the respect of New York crime boss John Gotti in 1989, when he allegedly led the murder conspiracy to kill Fred Weiss, the real estate developer. Palermo was later tied as well to the murder of DeCavalcante boss John D'Amato, but in both instances, there were no indictments or evidence.

Palermo managed to fly below the FBI's radar until the late 1990s, when federal authorities placed an informant inside the DeCavalcante family, and the man gained the confidence of one of his associates. In 1999, Palermo and a number of other members were indicted on a variety of charges, including murder, fraud, and labor racketeering. Palermo's response, which surprised both federal authorities and his confederates, was to agree to testify against his fellow mafiosi in exchange for a plea bargain. Like many other modern-day mobsters, he apparently decided it was better to give up his lifestyle rather than spend the rest of his life in jail—or risk the death penalty, which was a strong possibility in his case, given the nature and number of charges against him. Other mobsters who broke the code of silence said that they did so because the syndicate had decayed to the point where they just didn't respect it anymore.

Palermo, his appearance dramatically altered by hair dye and plastic surgery, testified against some of his fellow mafiosi before disappearing into the federal Witness Protection Program. During the trial of alleged mob leaders Philip Abramo, Guiseppe "Pino" Schifilliti, and Stefano Vitabile, Palermo reportedly exposed the influence that the Mafia had come to exert over the stock market.

An article in the May 18, 2003, *Sunday Times* reported that many investors who used mob-operated brokerage firms were "bullied into holding their shares even when they wanted to sell." This had escaped the notice of the stock market's financial overseers and resulted in billion-dollar profits for the Mafia.

Federal law enforcement records show that today there are about 25,000 members of organized crime in America, with approximately 250,000 affiliates scattered around the world. Overall, authorities believe that the Mafia's criminal activities generate more than $100 billion in annual income.

* * *

At the close of the twentieth century, New Jersey's wiseguys weren't the only criminals in business. On April 29, 1992, Sidney J. Reso, the president of Exxon International, was kidnapped outside his five-acre estate in Morris Township. The culprits proved to be Arthur Seale, a former Exxon employee, and his wife, Irene, who demanded an $18.5 million ransom for Reso's safe return. Their amateur foray into crime resulted in a jail term when Reso died during his captivity. Their reason for the kidnapping? Nothing more than greed. They had already squandered their own income several times over and felt that they deserved some easy money, as Reso apparently had more than enough to spare.

Two years later, Rabbi Fred Neulander of Cherry Hill allegedly hired two men to murder his wife, Carol. A prominent religious Reform leader who had started the M'kore Shalom Synagogue in 1974, Neulander was having an affair with Philadelphia radio personality Elaine Soncini and apparently believed that murder was his only alternative, because a divorce would have jeopardized his position in the community. Like Robert Marshall, Neulander chose to hire someone else to do his dirty work. But Leonard Jenoff, the private investigator he chose, eventually turned against his employer and became a key witness for the prosecution. Jenoff told authorities that the rabbi had agreed to pay him $30,000 to kill Mrs. Neulander, and that he and Paul Daniels, an unemployed Pennsauken man, beat her to death at her home. Although the rabbi proclaimed his innocence, he was found guilty and is currently serving a life sentence at the New Jersey State Prison in Trenton.

While state residents were shocked by both crimes, another horror occurred the same year that Carol Neulander was murdered. The rape and murder of young Megan Kanka was heart-rending, especially when it was discovered that the culprit responsible for the crime was living right across the street.

CHAPTER 7

The Death of Innocence

* * *

Is there anything more heinous than the death of a child at the hands of a sexual predator? When one New Jersey girl was tragically killed, her parents channeled their grief and anger into a campaign to try to make life safer for other children.

Like most suburban children, Megan Kanka's world was defined by specific boundaries. There was home, there was school, and then there was the neighborhood, where she whiled away the summer hours playing outside with her friends. But the neighborhood, which was supposed to be a safe haven—just like an extension of her home—proved one summer to be a jungle where dangerous predators lurked.

At age seven, Megan knew and trusted the people who lived around her. When she and her best friend, who lived next door, finished riding their bikes on July 29, 1994, the child went in for supper. Around 6:30 that Friday night, she apparently slipped out of the house to walk across the street to ask thirty-three-year-old Jesse Timmendequas about the boat he was washing in his driveway. Although he hadn't lived there long, he was a neighbor—no different in her eyes than anyone else who lived on Barbara Lee Drive. And so when Timmendequas invited her in to see his new puppy, Megan went. What child could resist the promise of a wriggling, joyful mass of fur to play with?

She was never seen alive again.

What no one in the quiet Hamilton Township neighborhood, including Maureen and Richard Kanka, realized at the time was that the house where their daughter disappeared was inhabited by not one, but three, convicted sex offenders. According to www.courttv.com, when Megan failed to respond to her mother's call a little later that fateful night, Maureen realized that her daughter was not in the house. She immediately called several other families in the neighborhood, but no one had seen Megan for some time. Moving quickly from house to house, Maureen asked Timmendequas, who lived diagonally across the street from the Kankas, if he had seen her daughter. Timmendequas said that he had seen Megan earlier that evening while he was working on his boat. Finally, when their search yielded no results, the Kankas realized they had no choice but to call the police. Megan was missing.

As darkness fell, the police conducted a door-to-door search of the neighborhood. At first they focused their attention on Joseph Cifelli, one of Timmendequas's roommates, after they learned he was a convicted sex offender. But their net quickly widened when they discovered that in addition to Cifelli, both Timmendequas and Brian Jenin, who also lived at the house owned by Cifelli's mother, were convicted sex offenders on parole. In fact, the three men had met at New Jersey's Avenel Adult Diagnostic and Treatment Center for sexual offenders. Cifelli and Jenin were able to produce an alibi—a receipt from an automatic bank teller machine that was stamped 6:34 P.M., the time of Megan's disappearance.

Timmendequas had no alibi.

Authorities found out that Timmendequas had two prior sex convictions involving young girls. In 1979, he had pleaded guilty to attempted aggravated sexual assault after an attack on a five-year-old girl in Piscataway. His sentence was suspended when he promised to go for counseling. But after Timmendequas ignored the court order, he had to serve nine months in the Middlesex Adult Correctional Center. Three years later, he was arrested in another assault involving a seven-year-old girl and pleaded guilty to attempted sexual contact and attempting to cause serious bodily injury in connection with the assault. On February 2, 1982, Timmendequas was sentenced to ten years at Avenel, but he was released after six years reportedly because of good behavior and time served. When he was free, Timmendequas moved to Hamilton Township to room with Cifelli and Jenin.

No one knows how many pedophiles—people who prey on children—live in the United States today. And the advent of the Internet has allowed them easy access to the sordid world of child pornography that some psychologists feel helps fuel their desires, placing children in their vicinity at risk. Pedophiles come from a variety of socioeconomic backgrounds. In recent years, the Catholic Church has been rocked by charges of past instances of child abuse among the clergy, while Michael Jackson, the former "King of Pop," fled the country to avoid further prosecution on charges of sexual assault. Although some illnesses can be controlled with medication or a change of lifestyle, to date there is no known cure to stop those who attack children. And it seemed that Timmendequas, despite having undergone extensive counseling, was one of those predators who had not changed his ways.

A few hours after local authorities had been contacted, hundreds of volunteers, including off-duty police, firefighters, and search-and-rescue dog teams from throughout New Jersey and Pennsylvania, gathered to search a three-mile radius around Megan's house. They canvassed the town, handing out Megan's pictures, as the New Jersey State Police conducted a search from the air. Friends and neighbors willingly allowed the search teams to enter their yards in an effort to help find the child. While the community rallied around them, the Kankas made a televised plea for their daughter's safe return. But unknown to the family, it was already too late.

Experienced law enforcement officers know that someone who is overeager to assist an investigation is sometimes worth extra attention. They soon noted that though Timmendequas was extremely nervous in their presence, he was willing to accompany the officers to police headquarters for questioning. According to www.crimelibrary.com, he admitted to authorities that he had been "getting those feelings" again for little girls. When the child was still missing on the following day, Timmendequas allegedly confessed that he had killed Megan after she tried to resist his advances once they were inside the house. At one point, the child struck her head on a dresser in his bedroom, and he was afraid that drops of her blood would incriminate him in the assault. He covered her head with plastic, then strangled her with a belt. He led police to the child's body, which had been thrown into an overgrown stretch of grass in a nearby county park.

Timmendequas was charged with murder, two counts of felony murder, kidnapping, and four counts of aggravated sexual assault. Prosecutors charged that after luring Megan into his house, he raped her, then strangled her by placing two plastic bags over her head. The state added that Timmendequas gratuitously killed Megan to prevent her from telling anyone what he had done. Authorities said that Timmendequas then placed the child's body in an old toy box, which he carried out of the house to his truck. After he took the dead child to the park, he sexually assaulted her again before he returned home to wash down his truck, the toy box, and the steps to his house.

On November 19, 1994, Timmendequas pleaded not guilty to the charges against him in Superior Court and was scheduled for trial. Since the case had attracted a lot of media attention, the jury pool was selected from Hunterdon County. After the two-week-long trial began before Superior Court Judge Andrew J. Smithson in May

1997, Deputy First Assistant Mercer County Prosecutor Kathryn Flicker and Assistant Prosecutor Lewis Korngut called seventeen witnesses to testify against the defendant. The defense team, attorneys Roy B. Greenman and Assistant Public Defender Barbara Lependorf, called in a social worker and a psychologist during the course of the trial to testify that Timmendequas's troubled life had a direct impact on his actions. They maintained that during his childhood, the accused had been victimized by domestic violence, substance abuse, and emotional and physical neglect, as well as sexual abuse. The prosecution brought in their own experts to challenge these statements, however, and no friend or family member ever came forward to speak on his behalf. In fact, his father later denied all of Timmendequas's claims and stated that his son deserved the death penalty for his crimes.

When Maureen Kanka was called to the stand, she told the court that the defendant had seen her and other family members searching the neighborhood for Megan. Maureen testified that he said he saw the little girl going to visit a friend. She recounted how she later identified her daughter at the morgue. When it became difficult for veteran detectives to testify about finding Megan's body, Timmendequas's lawyers asked the court for a mistrial because, they said, too much emotion was bound to taint the jury's opinion of their client. Smithson denied their appeal, but he ordered the prosecution to try to keep the witnesses under control.

Detectives from Hamilton Township and the New Jersey State Police testified that Timmendequas confessed five times, both verbally and in writing, that he strangled and raped Megan. They said that he led them the following day to Megan's partially clad body in the park three miles from Barbara Lee Drive. Mercer County Medical Examiner Dr. Raafat Ahmad added to the damaging testimony when she provided an autopsy report that showed that Megan had been horribly battered before she was strangled and raped.

During the trial, Court TV was allowed to tape the attorneys' opening and closing statements and, finally, the verdict when it was handed down by the jury. Despite the best efforts of Timmendequas's attorneys to generate sympathy for their client, the jury was not moved by the horror stories from his past. On May 30, 1997, he was found guilty of all counts, including capital murder. During the penalty phase of the sentencing, which was held the following week, the jury sentenced him to the death penalty for his crimes. According to www.cnn.com, the six-man, six-woman jury deliberated for more than ten hours over a two-day stretch but, in the end, unanimously decided that Timmendequas merited death by lethal injection instead of life in prison without parole. Although the panel found that Timmendequas had not planned his horrible crime and had shown remorse for his action, they felt that this did not mitigate the fact that he had callously murdered Megan to avoid arrest for her kidnap and rape. He was immediately sentenced to death by Judge Smithson and removed to the death row complex at the New Jersey State Prison.

According to an article in the June 21, 1997, *Star-Ledger:*

As the verdict was read, the 36-year-old pedophile, whose crime stunned a nation and sparked dozens of laws aimed at protecting children from sexual predators, seemed to quake. His head shook and he chewed anxiously on a white breath mint as his attorney placed a hand on his shoulder. Before he was led from the room for the short ride to death row at New Jersey State Prison a few blocks from the Mercer County Courthouse, the judge pronounced him "the most publicly despised and vilified individual this court recalls in the state of New Jersey."

The judge set August 1 as the date of execution, but Timmendequas—like all criminals convicted of capital crimes—was automatically entitled to an appeal. He was still sitting in solitary confinement on death row as of this writing.

Not knowing that almost a decade would pass and still Timmendequas would remain alive, the Kankas cried with relief at the verdict. After the trial, Maureen Kanka said she was gratified by the decision, but the family's suffering remained undiminished. As reported on www.cnn.com: "We asked the prosecutor's office to go for the maximum and we never wavered from those initial thoughts," said Richard Kanka. "This deserves the maximum penalty allowed by law, and with the help of Kathryn Flicker, we got it." According to Flicker, even if Timmendequas is never executed by the state, he has been permanently removed from the streets and the possibility of ever harming another child.

The New Jersey State Supreme Court, in a split ruling in 1999, upheld his conviction and verdict. Two years later, the Supreme Court once again upheld Timmendequas's conviction in a four-to-one ruling, stating that the penalty was fair.

Almost immediately after Megan's murder, the Kankas started a grassroots campaign, using donations that poured in from concerned supporters, to enact legislation requiring all sex offenders to register with the police, who in turn must notify the neighbors when they move into a community. The legislation, christened Megan's Law, is modeled after similar laws that were established in Oregon. Although some contended that it was unconstitutional, Megan's Law was upheld in 1995 by the New Jersey State Supreme Court. The following year, the federal government passed its own version, titled the Jacob Wetterling Crimes Against Children Law. By 1997, all states were required to pass their own versions of Megan's Law or risk losing federal funding.

To date, more than forty-five states, plus the District of Columbia, have passed legislation requiring convicted sex offenders to notify the police of their presence. The federal statute allows individual states to decide what the level of risk is for each offender and whether community members must be notified. Although there have been periodic challenges against the law since that time, sex offenders in New Jersey must notify authorities for the rest of their lives when they move into a community. Offenders considered low-risk are only required to tell the police where they live. Information on medium-risk offenders has to be shared with day-care centers and schools. If high-risk offenders move into an area, then anyone they might encounter should be warned of their presence. In New Jersey, risk is determined by the number of offenses committed, the age of the victim, whether a weapon was used, and whether the offender has successfully completed therapy.

Unfortunately, Megan's Law is sometimes ignored by the offenders, who don't always feel compelled to obey. In 2003, twenty-three convicted sex offenders were arrested in Hackensack for failing to register with the police when they moved into the area. What is chilling is that the prosecutor's office said eight more remained fugitives, who may still be at large. In 2006, five convicted sex offenders were indicted by an Atlantic County grand jury for the same offense. That same year, a registered sex offender challenged Lower Township's 2005 ordinance that banned him from living within 500 feet of public areas or 25 feet of school bus stops. His case is supported by a number of groups, including the American Civil Liberties Union, which claims that the ordinance violates the New Jersey State Constitution.

Some argue that the provisions called for in Megan's Law are simply too harsh and too reactionary—that it is not possible to completely protect children from sexual predators, and that greater danger exists within the family than from strangers. But it is believed that there are more than 100,000 pedophiles in the United States who are not registered, and according to statistics provided by the U.S. Justice Department, such offenders are four times more likely to be arrested for repeat crimes. Until sweeping changes are enacted in the criminal justice system, which often hands out nominal sentences for assaulting a child, parents and legal guardians can arm themselves with copies of Megan's Law, which may be obtained from all county prosecutors' offices throughout New Jersey.

The house where Timmendequas and his roommates lived was purchased after the trial by the local Rotary for $105,000. The organization then tore it down and created a small park, planted with pink flowers, that was christened Megan's Place.

Although the years since Megan's death have been difficult at times, the Kankas have focused on their goal of making sure other families never have to suffer the same type of loss. The family established the Megan Nicole Kanka Foundation in 1994 to assist all parents and legal guardians in protecting their children from sexual predators. For further information, contact the foundation at P.O. Box 9956, Trenton, NJ 08650, telephone (609) 890-2201, e-mail meganfoundation@optline.net, or visit the website www.megan nicolekankafoundation.org.

* * *

Three short years after the tragic death of young Megan Kanka, Garden State residents were startled by the sudden appearance of a midwestern spree killer named Andrew Cunanan, a twenty-seven-year-old who was fleeing authorities for the murders of four men. Although he would eventually become best known as the murderer of noted fashion designer Gianni Versace, Cunanan didn't leave New Jersey without taking a life. On May 9, 1997, he murdered forty-five-year-old William Reese, the caretaker of the Finn's Point cemetery in rural Salem County. Reese, a history buff who had founded a local Civil War reenactment group, was shot by the fugitive, who stole Reese's 1995 red Chevrolet pickup truck and disappeared south. Cunanan eventually surfaced in Florida, where he killed Versace and, on a houseboat in Miami, took one final victim—himself.

CHAPTER 8
Law Enforcement

✳ ✳ ✳

While the focus of this book has been the villains and monsters who commit crimes against their fellow citizens, this chapter looks a little more closely at the women and men at the opposite end of the spectrum—the police officers who protect and serve on both the state and local levels. Although they are supported by a network of other law enforcement professionals, including prosecutors, prison guards, and judges, the police officers are the ones who respond at all hours, under all conditions, when someone dials 911.

Becoming a police officer is often a thankless job. The hours are long, the shift changes are difficult for family life, and many departments are understaffed and underequipped to meet the demands they face. Since the 1920s, hundreds of New Jersey police officers have been killed or wounded in the line of duty. Yet for every member of the thin blue line who falls, another comes along to take that person's place. This small group of dedicated men and women who work in state and local police departments are usually the first line of defense against crime for most New Jersey residents. Many of them rushed to the aid of their fellow officers in New York City on September 11, 2001. These officers, the "first responders" who protect our lives, property, and even parks and forests, are frequently called upon to serve informally as mediators and psychologists in addition to enforcing the law. Although many of them retire without ever having to draw a gun, anyone who is on the job knows that the potential for violence is always there.

So what prompts someone to accept the challenge of this dangerous field?

Although he could pass at first glance for a high school senior, twenty-nine-year-old Terry Hall is a three-year veteran of the Vineland Police Department. He couldn't imagine doing anything else for a living, because being a police officer is something he's dreamed about since childhood.

"My family had a close friend who was in the Millville Police Department," says Hall, who was born and raised in nearby Millville. "He would always come over to the house in his patrol car and I'd be looking out the window, waiting. My parents always knew I wanted to be a police officer, because I had the TV show *Cops* on every Saturday night. It was no surprise for them."

Still, after high school, Hall explored the idea of becoming an elementary school teacher. At the time, the profession was attempting to recruit more men, and Hall liked the idea of working with children. He started pursuing an associate's degree at Cumberland County College, but those plans changed soon after he began a full-time job as an emergency medical technician on the Millville Rescue Squad. He answered 911 calls for three years before being promoted to supervisor. Rescue work brought him in contact with a number of Millville officers, who encouraged him to begin working part-time at the police department. For the next two years, Hall divided his time between the rescue squad and the police department, and he realized that his love of law enforcement was still strong. At that point, he decided to try to find full-time police work, if not for Millville, then with another local department.

When Vineland began to recruit more officers, Hall moved there because of the opportunity to work full-time. In October 2002, he was delighted to find that he ranked number four on the law enforcement Civil Service Examination, and shortly afterward, he began training in the Police Academy at Sea Girt. Hall recalls his first night on the job after graduating from the academy: "I had to ride with the field supervisor because all of the other training supervisors were tied up. And the first call I went on was 'shots fired.' A guy got shot in the stomach. After six years as an EMT, the sight of blood—of gunshot wounds—was nothing new to me. Of course, then I was in the medical role, but now I was in the police role, and it was totally different. That was just a little eye-opener, and that was just the first night."

The patrol areas in Vineland are broken into sections that differ according to the number of officers on a shift, says Hall. Normally there are twenty officers covering twenty different assigned areas, but that number can fluctuate if someone is out sick or on vacation. Although they normally work alone, the officers are quick to respond out of their area if a fellow officer needs assistance. Verbal threats and physical violence have become more common than they were in years past, as road rage and gang activity have increased. If the patrol officers respond to a scene where a homicide or another major crime has occurred, they generate an initial report of what they discover at the site and contact their shift supervisor, who then contacts the detectives if further investigation is required. The only time Vineland officers work with partners is in the event of a special function or if the roads are snowy.

Hall considers himself fortunate to be a patrol officer. He works a steady four days from 9:30 A.M. to 8 P.M., then has four days off. Although most people wouldn't enjoy working more than ten hours a day, he considers his schedule less stressful than those of the spe-

POLITICALLY INCORRECT

Corruption in politics dates back to the earliest years of European settlement. According to Marc Mappen in *Jerseyana: The Underside of New Jersey History,* the first recorded bribe in the state occurred in 1703, after Edward Hyde, Lord Cornbury, first cousin to Queen Anne of England, used his family connections to assume the position of royal governor of the colony of New York, then was given control of the New Jersey territory as well.

When Cornbury arrived in the New World, his primary concern was to see how he could personally benefit from his dual appointment. When a handful of New Jersey tenants and landlords asked him to arbitrate a dispute over property rights, Cornbury threw his support behind the property owners—especially after they threw £100 his way. In the four years that followed, Cornbury and his entourage, known as the Cornbury Ring, made enemies among both the rich and the poor, because they were always willing to sell their support to the highest bidder. But it seems that Cornbury's greed wasn't his only vice. In addition to a penchant for alcohol, he had a habit of periodically dressing in women's clothing and walking through town—a habit that was generally not well received at that time.

Out of patience with her cousin's excesses, Queen Anne recalled Cornbury to England in 1708. Before he could return, however, the governor was arrested in New York and jailed for nonpayment of debts. Ironically, while Cornbury was in prison, his father died and he inherited the title of earl of Clarendon. Because his new rank provided enough money to pay off his debts, Cornbury fled back to England, where he apparently enjoyed a long and distinguished public career.

cial units, which alternate round-the-clock shifts. At the same time, he eagerly anticipates the day when he can join the Street Crimes Division, which is responsible for taking drug dealers and other criminals off Vineland's streets.

Once a semi-rural suburban community where folks shopped downtown on Landis Avenue, Vineland has grown dramatically in

But corruption apparently still thrived in 1905, when Lincoln Steffens wrote an article for *McClure's* in which he dubbed New Jersey "the traitor state" because special business interest groups, notably the owners of railroad lines, were unduly influencing state officials. Mappen noted in his book that "when rival railroads wanted to build lines in the state, they had to buy their own politicians." At a time when the "robber barons" were losing public support, New Jersey officials allowed them to maintain corporate headquarters in the state. In addition, the Corporation Trust Company of New Jersey, established by attorney James B. Dill, helped them through the state's incorporation process, then shielded them from government regulations.

Reformers in the state were thrilled when Woodrow Wilson was elected governor in 1910, because he forced bills through the legislature that effectively closed down the Corporation Trust Company and established strict controls over those companies that were already in business within New Jersey. Unfortunately, Wilson's efforts proved a mixed and not-so-long-lasting blessing. The corporations simply relocated, and ten years later, all of his bills were repealed. New Jersey returned to the business of business, with lobbyists looking to grease all the necessary wheels.

Soon afterward, New Jersey residents elected a Republican governor, Harold G. Hoffman, who served from 1935 to 1938. He was considered such a poor statesman that his own political party turned against him. At the time of his death in 1954, it was discovered that Hoffman had been on the take throughout his political career. His unofficial activities as governor had included embezzling $300,000 from a bank in South Amboy.

recent years. Housing developments built on the site of once-prosperous farmland have brought hundreds of new residents to the city, straining its infrastructure. With that growth, the town has seen an increase in crime. Urban street gangs from New York and Philadelphia have relocated to the area. Although police have managed to reduce the incidents of auto theft, burglary, and assault, the number of rapes and murders have more than doubled between 2001 and 2003. Whereas the U.S. average in 2003 for crime is 329.7, according to www.city-data.com, when all the numbers for Vineland are compiled, the city's figure for that year is 456.8.

At the same time, the Vineland Police Department is growing and changing to meet these increased needs. In 2006, veteran police chief Mario Brunetta retired after forty-three years on the job. He was replaced by Tim Codispoti, who joined the department in 1983. Under Codispoti's leadership, the city has hired five new officers, bringing the total to 150—the largest police department in Vineland's history. In addition to their normal duties, the officers' responsibilities include an active Police Athletic League program; the Police Explorers, for children between eleven and eighteen; special education units; and an in-school drug awareness program. The department is also planning to start its own canine unit.

Although Vineland does not require officers to hold a degree, Hall expects to return to college someday. But the focus of his studies this time will be criminal justice, not elementary education. When he's not at work, he enjoys spending time at the gym or socializing with other officers, discussing the day's events. "It seems like even when your shift is over, the work isn't really done, because when we see each other, we usually start talking about the calls we've gone on. That's because we're like a brotherhood. The only one who really understands what we do is another officer."

Although they are not affiliated with a single municipality, the New Jersey State Police face challenges similar to, and sometimes greater than, those of municipal officers. While people tend to think of the state police in terms of speeding tickets or other traffic violations, state officers, like their municipal counterparts, are often required to play a variety of law enforcement roles.

Just ask New Jersey State Police Lieutenant Thomas Macauley. At age forty-four, the Mickleton resident has spent half his life with the state police. Now married with four children, Macauley graduated from Sea Girt in 1985 after completing the State Police Department's six-month training program. He started out as a trooper, patrolling the backroads of South Jersey, then later moved on to other units, including Major Crimes, Corruption, Missing Persons, and Statewide Intelligence Management. He currently serves as supervisor of the Major Crimes Unit. When he's not on the job, he also teaches criminal justice and related computer courses as an adjunct professor for Fairleigh Dickinson University and works as an instructor for the National Center for Missing and Exploited Children police training programs.

Macauley, who knew that he wanted to be a police officer at age fourteen, holds a bachelor's degree in criminal justice from Temple University and a master's degree in public administration from Rutgers University. He started his career as a municipal police officer in Woodlynne but moved to the state level because he felt the job would be more challenging. "I wanted to work statewide, not be confined to one municipality," Macauley says. "And our agency is diverse; not only do we have general police duties in a variety of areas, we also work covert and undercover investigations throughout New Jersey and sometimes into other states." The veteran trooper believes that part of New Jersey's problems with crimes lie in the state's proximity to Philadelphia and New York City.

The father of four enjoys focusing on the details that can sometimes make or break an investigation. But the job isn't for everybody. He thinks that working for the state police can be more demanding, because officers need college degrees in order to advance, and their cases sometimes cross a variety of jurisdictions, from the local to federal level. Macauley has investigated crimes that were tried in state and federal courts.

His worst moment on the job involved the discovery in 1991 of a body that had been dissected into six pieces, with half discovered in one location and the remainder ninety miles away. Also difficult were the murder case of a child in the Cape May region and being assigned to northern New Jersey immediately after the tragedy of September 11, 2001. He counts among his best moments helping resolve a twenty-one-year-old murder case, breaking up a major auto theft ring based in Newark, and investigating a superior court judge who was eventually prosecuted.

Macauley plans to retire some time in the next ten years, and he hopes that new recruits will properly arm themselves with an education before joining the state police. With the advent of the Internet and an increase in white-collar crime, he advises pursuing college degrees in areas such as computer science or accounting, with an eye toward a graduate degree, to be better prepared for the demands of the job.

The officers employed at county sheriffs' departments and the New Jersey Department of Environmental Protection, known as the State Park Police, may be primarily employed in slightly different capacities, but they undergo the same training as both state and municipal officers at police training academies. As a result, they are authorized to issue summonses, investigate crimes, or make arrests when necessary. The State Park Police sometimes face some unique problems, however. Unlike those of other departments, their territory often consists of thousands of acres of dense forest riddled with hidden trails through the underbrush that are not always easy to follow.

In recent years, many police departments from the state to local level are using the Internet as a tool to raise the public's awareness about child predators, fugitives, and other criminals, as well as educate people about everything from water safety to traffic jams. In addition, they frequently share staff and technology with other departments as a means of improving communication and resolving crimes. In 2006, the New Jersey State Police purchased a small, unmanned submarine equipped with a robotic claw that can be used to search for objects underwater. This remote-operated vehicle (ROV) may be borrowed by any law enforcement agency in New Jersey to pursue a criminal investigation.

Such interagency cooperation is always valuable, especially as it appears that New Jersey will continue to endure its share of criminal activity for years to come. Areas such as Essex County are recognized, in fact, as places where it's possible to literally get away with murder. Roughly a third of all killings in the Garden State take place in Newark and other densely populated, gang-ridden cities such as Irvington and East Orange. Statistics gathered by the *Star-Ledger,* a regional newspaper, revealed that of the 637 murders that occurred between 1998 and 2003 in Essex County, less that half of them were solved. In many instances, witnesses either disappeared or were intimidated into recanting their testimonies. In cases where the murderers were captured, they usually were sentenced to less than the mandated thirty-year minimum because of plea bargaining.

The criminal justice system is undoubtedly frustrating for police officers, who are sometimes criticized for allegedly using force or other behavior that some deem unacceptable. But what some of the critics fail to acknowledge is that most people don't have to put their lives on the line when they go to work. The stress and frustration of the job can occasionally take their toll—especially when the police find that the people they hoped to remove from the streets are soon out of jail and right back to their old habits again.

That doesn't mean the prisons aren't filled, though. According to statistics from the New Jersey Department of Corrections, there were close to 6,000 inmates in 1975. By 2000, that number had more than quadrupled, to 28,000. Approximately 75 percent of all prisoners in New Jersey are from less than half of the counties. They often come from low-income urban centers with few opportunities for employment or education. In 2005, the *New York Times* reported that "New Jersey had the most crowded prison system in the country, according to the Justice Department, operating at 143 percent of capacity." Prisoners are regularly released from jail once their sentences are served, but it seems that two out of three are usually rearrested within three years.

With such frightening statistics, it is not surprising that some people believe that those who commit crimes aren't just bad, but evil. And, they feel that evil is running rampant throughout the world. Dr. Michael Weiner, a forensic psychiatrist and founder of the Forensic Panel, has developed the Depravity Scale, an instrument designed to present an objective perspective on criminal behavior. According to www.crimelibrary.com, Weiner feels that a jury's response to a case is sometimes swayed by crimes being described with terms such as "cruel, wanton, vile, cold-blooded, outrageous, or monstrous." He thinks that his system, which measures the offender's ability to choose a deliberate action, provides a better scale for deciding the fate of the accused. According to Weiner, who believes evil does exist, scientists have a responsibility to better define the term in hopes of effecting positive changes someday. There is no single explanation for why such evil exists and its impact on criminal behavior.

Not every person who watches violent movies like *Texas Chainsaw Massacre* or *American Psycho,* which examine the psyches of serial killers, will be inspired to act out such sadistic fantasies. Whether the cause is psychological, emotional, environmental, or just a lack of something that keeps the rest of the population from breaking the law, it is unlikely that psychiatrists and other students of human behavior will resolve the question anytime soon.

Epilogue

As a native of the Garden State, I have tried to share just one aspect of New Jersey's unique personality. Unfortunately, crimes undoubtedly will continue to be committed throughout the state, from the smallest town to the largest metropolis. Some incidents will be readily resolved. Others will linger for years before the criminals, like Charles Cullen, are brought to justice. Cullen was a New Jersey nurse who admitted to killing at least forty patients since he started his career in 1987. In 2006, Cullen was sentenced to eleven consecutive life terms in prison. The forty-six-year-old used lethal doses of different medicines, including digoxin, to kill patients ranging from twenty-one to eighty-nine years of age. He worked undetected at close to a dozen different health-care facilities because they reportedly failed to share employment records.

By now it's obvious that unlike in the movies, real crimes are not always easily resolved. Although knowing that criminals live among us may seem a little overwhelming at times, I have faith that the majority of my fellow New Jerseyans will continue to behave responsibly.

Just don't forget to lock the doors.

Exploring New Jersey's Criminal History

Anyone who is interested in learning more about New Jersey's criminal past should make time to visit the Burlington County Jail in Mount Holly and the New Jersey State Police Museum in Trenton, which offer some fascinating insight into the Garden State's history of crime.

The Burlington County Jail, an imposing three-story structure, is open to the public these days as a museum. Guided tours of the facility take visitors behind the walls for a close-up look at the cells and copies of inmate graffiti that have been preserved and are exhibited throughout the building. The prison yard was once the site of public hangings on gallows that were erected there. Entire families would travel to the site to witness the executions. Up until it closed in 1965, Burlington County was the oldest continually operating prison in the United States. Located at the intersection of Route 541 and Grant Street in Mount Holly, the jail is open Mondays through Saturdays from 10 A.M. to 4 P.M. and Sundays from noon to 4 P.M. For directions or further information, call (609) 518-7667.

The New Jersey State Police Museum documents the eighty-five-year history of the state police, formed in 1921 under the direction of twenty-five-year-old Col. H. Norman Schwarzkopf. After completing training at Sea Girt, which is still home to the police training academy, 81 recruits out of a class of 120 began patrolling the rural communities of New Jersey on December 5 of that year. According to the New Jersey State Police website, the first two barracks were Troop A, which was stationed in Hammonton, and Troop B, assigned to Netcong.

A tour of the museum starts with an introductory video, followed by exhibits that illustrate how state troopers are trained. A highlight of the tour is original artifacts from the sensational Lindbergh kidnapping, including ransom notes, the ladder used by the kidnapper, and a video of the *Fox Movietone News* showing footage of the "Trial of the Century." Other exhibits focus on early police facilities, transportation, weaponry, and the Police Marine Bureau. A forensic science exhibit explains modern lab techniques for identifying fingerprints and DNA samples, processes that have become integral parts of police procedures. Visitors have the opportunity to view their own fingerprints with interactive microscopes to learn more about how this procedure works.

The museum is open Mondays through Saturdays from 10 A.M. to 4 P.M. Group tours are available by appointment. For directions and further information, call (609) 882-2000, extension 6400.

Bibliography

Books

Ahlgren, Gregory, and Stephen Monier. *Crime of the Century: The Lindbergh Kidnapping Hoax.* Boston: Branden Books, 1993.

Anastasia, George. *Blood and Honor: Inside the Scarfo Mob—the Mafia's Most Violent Family.* Philadelphia: Camino Books, 2004.

Benford, Timothy B., and James P. Johnson. *Righteous Carnage: The List Murders.* New York: Charles Scribner's Sons, 1991.

Camisa, Harry. *Inside Out: Fifty Years Behind the Walls of New Jersey's Trenton State Prison.* Windsor, NJ: Windsor Press, 2003.

Cunningham, John T., and Donald A. Sinclair. *Murder Did Pay: 19th Century New Jersey Murders.* Newark: New Jersey Historical Society, 1982.

Davis, Ed. *Atlantic City Diary: A Century of Memories, 1880-1985.* McKee City, NJ: Atlantic Sunrise Publishing Co., 1980.

Fisher, Jim. *The Ghosts of Hopewell: Setting the Record Straight in the Lindbergh Case.* Carbondale: Southern Illinois University Press, 1999.

Genovese, Peter. *New Jersey Curiosities: Quirky Characters, Roadside Oddities and Other Offbeat Stuff.* Guilford, CT: Globe Pequot Press, 2003.

Grun, Bernard. *The Timetables of History.* New York: Simon and Schuster, 1979.

Johnson, Nelson. *Boardwalk Empire: The Birth, High Times, and Corruption of Atlantic City.* Medford, NJ: Plexus Publishing, 2002.

Jones, Ann. *Women Who Kill.* New York: Holt, Rinehart and Winston, 1980.

Mappen, Marc. *Jerseyana: The Underside of New Jersey History.* New Brunswick, NJ: Rutgers University Press, 1992.

Martinelli, Patricia A., and Charles A. Stansfield, Jr. *Haunted New Jersey: Ghosts and Strange Phenomena of the Garden State.* Mechanicsburg, PA: Stackpole Books, 2004.

McGinnis, Joe. *Blind Faith.* New York: G. P. Putnam's Sons, 1989.

Pileggi, Nicholas. *Wise Guy: Life in a Mafia Family.* New York: Pocket Books, 1985.

Schreiber, Flora Rheta. *The Shoemaker: The Anatomy of a Psychotic.* New York: Simon and Schuster, 1983.

Smith, Greg B. *Made Men: The True Rise-and-Fall Story of a New Jersey Mob Family.* New York: Berkley Books, 2003.

Tomlinson, Gerald. *Murdered in Jersey.* New Brunswick, NJ: Rutgers University Press, 2001.

———. *Seven Jersey Murders.* XLibris, 2003.

Vecoli, Rudolph J. *The People of New Jersey.* Princeton, NJ: D. Van Nostrand Company, 1965.

Works Progress Administration Federal Writers' Project. *New Jersey: A Guide to Its Present and Past.* New York: Hastings House, 1946.

Websites

www.crimelibrary.com

www.capitalcentury.com/1939.html

www.ccadp.org/electricchair.htm

www.TheOldenTimes.com

www.dailyjournal.com

www.wikipedia.org

www.law.umkc.edu

www.co.cumberland.nj.us

www.nj.com

www.city-data.com

www.wnbc.com

www.njreporter.org

www.opinionjournal.com

www.washtimes.com

www.politics.nexcess.net

www.pressofatlanticcity.com

www.dumb.com

www.southjerseynews.com

www.mafianj.com

www.skcentral.com

www.ocoserver.com

www.onewal.com

www.history.acusd.edu

www.AmericanMafia.com

www.memory.loc.gov

Acknowledgments

I thank my editor, Kyle Weaver, for his continued support in developing this book from idea to reality, and editorial assistant Amy Cooper for her meticulous attention to detail in preparing the final manuscript. In addition, my thanks go to archivist Mark Falzini at the New Jersey State Police Museum, Officer Terry Hall of the Vineland Police Department, and Lt. Thomas Macauley of the New Jersey State Police for providing their professional insights into crime. I am grateful to my friend Tony Ficcaglia for sharing his knowledge of psychology and the late Gerald Tomlinson, a talented writer, for teaching me much about the subject of murder. The dedicated staff of the Vineland Public Library has once again earned my eternal gratitude for patiently fielding all my interlibrary loan requests. And finally, a heartfelt thank you to the men and women who work in law enforcement throughout New Jersey for their selfless dedication to an often difficult profession.